Following Jesus in the Hindu Context

Be thou, my soul, a house of prayer,
A beauteous seat for the abode
Of the all-holy Spirit of God,
Throned in triumphant power there.

(Tilak: *Christayana* 1:105)

Narayan Vaman Tilak and
his wife Lakshmibai Tilak

Following Jesus in the Hindu Context

The Intriguing Implications of
N. V. Tilak's Life and Thought

H. L. Richard

William Carey Library
Pasadena, California

Copyright 1998 by H. L. Richard

This is a new edition, adapted for western readers, of the book *Christ-Bhakti: Narayan Vaman Tilak and Christian Work among Hindus*, 2nd revised and expanded Indian edition of 1998 (Secunderabad, India: OM Books). The first Indian edition, 1991, was published by ISPCK, Delhi.

Picture opposite title page: courtesy of the publishers of *Sampurna Smrutichitre*, Popular Prakashan (Mumbai, India). Poem on initial page: from Narayan Vaman Tilak's epic poem on Christ, *Christayana*, published in his book, *Bhakti Niranjana* (Nasik, India: Nagarik Press, n.d.), p. 18; trans. J. C. Winslow. Cover design by Melissa and Kent Lawson.

Published by William Carey Library
P.O. Box 40129, Pasadena, California 91114   (626) 798-0819

Library of Congress Cataloging-in-Publication Data

Richard, H. L.
    Following Jesus in the Hindu context: the intriguing implications of N.V. Tilak's life and thought / by H. L. Richard.
        p.   cm.
    Rev. ed. of: Christ-bhakti. 2nd rev. and expanded Indian ed. 1998.
    Includes bibliographical references and index.
    ISBN 0-87808-288-3 (alk. paper)
    1. Tilak, Narayan Vaman, 1862?–1919. 2. Converts from Hinduism—Biography. 3. Missions to Hindus—India. I. Richard, H. L. Christ-bhakti. II. Title.

BV3269.T57R53   1998
248.2'46'092—dc21
[B]   98-46314
                                                             CIP

Printed in the United States of America

To my wife

without whose support
this could not
have been written

Delhi

Dwarka

Bombay

Ahmadnagar

Pandharpur

Calcutta

India

0   200   400   KM
0   100   200   300   MILES

Contents

Abstract

N. V. Tilak's place as one of the outstanding pioneers of Protestant mission history is documented. Tilak was born in 1861 in western India in a Brahmin family. He was an ardent nationalist and a gifted poet who put his faith in Christ and was baptized into the Christian church in 1895. As an unusually gifted individual Tilak was never fully at home within the westernized systems of church and mission life in India. He was a pioneer in adapting Hindu forms for the expression of biblical faith, particularly through his devotional songs and a never-completed epic poem on the life of Christ. He went yet further by resigning in 1917, after 21 years in mission service, and entering the fourth stage in traditional Brahmin life, *sannyasa* or renunciation. In this last brief stage of his life Tilak saw himself as an apostle to India and sought to gather a fellowship of both baptized and unbaptized disciples of Jesus. No one has yet surpassed his efforts at contextualization of biblical faith for the Hindu world. All interested in contextual Christian communication will want to study this remarkable figure.

Key words: missions, contextualization, evangelism, Hinduism, India, biography, poet, hymns, Christianity in India, religious order, brotherhood, *sannyasa*, caste, patriotism, conversion, Indian theology, fulfillment, communication.

Foreword

People will turn to this absorbing study of N. V. Tilak for a number of reasons. Some, interested in the history of the church in India, will come to read the biography of a fascinating but relatively neglected pioneer. Others may be drawn by his reputation as a major Marathi poet and hymn writer of the devotional life. The Marathi hymn book includes more than 200 of his compositions. Still others will find themselves attracted by his Christian version of pre-Gandhian nationalism, his efforts to promote "an Indian church on genuinely Indian lines."

There will also be readers who come with more sophisticated questions. And the questions may, for some, even strongly resemble suspicions. Some may be looking for answers to more contemporary issues. How closely was Tilak tied to early ideas of Jesus Christ as the fulfillment of Hinduism? Would Tilak have been willing to speak of "the unknown Christ of Hinduism" as some do today? What did Tilak mean when he referred to the great Hindu *bhakti* poet, Tukaram, and said that he had journeyed by the bridge of Tukaram to the feet of Christ? Did he see Christ at work in Hinduism in a hidden way?

I have found in this biography of Tilak the story of a Christian struggling with his context and with the ever-present issue of how to lift up Jesus in the uniqueness of that context. How can this be done in such a way that the biblical Jesus speaks and the world of Hinduism hears? Current writers sometimes call this *contextualization*. It is a very long word for a very old problem—the communication of the good news that Jesus saves to a cultural world with its own definitions of salvation.

For those who think this question of context is a new one, this biography will serve as a good reminder of how long we Christians have struggled with it and how long India's Christians in particular have struggled with it. In a time when too many of India's missionaries perceived of Hinduism as only a dark universe "where all life dies and death lives," Tilak was part of that core of Christian believers who looked for more rays of light than were usually found then.

Did he find more light than a biblical perspective allows? Can his struggle to understand and interpret the Christian faith in a Hindu world aid us today? Do we find in his Christian poetry some of the first efforts at hermeneutics that later scholars will call the seeds of theology? How can we speak of Jesus as "guru of the world"?

This book is an exciting step in examining the Christian past to aid the Christian future. One does not have to agree with all its twists and turns to recognize the help it offers. But surely all of us must recognize the challenge it makes.

Harvie M. Conn
Professor of Missions
Westminster Seminary
Philadelphia, Penn., USA

Preface

India has produced no greater Christian than N. V. Tilak and all of church history internationally reveals few figures as great. Yet since his death in 1919 only two significant biographical studies have been published (both now largely unknown or forgotten) and no analytical study of importance has yet appeared. This book begins to put right this serious oversight.

There is no better starting point for a study of the Christian attitude and approach to Hinduism than the life of Tilak. As a convert from Brahminical Hinduism Tilak had inside knowledge and experience of Hindu life and thought. In Christ he grew in understanding of what it means to be "all things to all men" (1 Cor. 9:22). He stands first among Protestant Christians who made efforts at contextual understanding of and approaches to Hindus. Recently renewed interest in this field from both Protestants and Roman Catholics has brought Tilak's name often into discussion and writing. Yet a deeply studied analysis of his life is not available.

Tilak's greatness and continued significance for contextually sharing Christ with Hindus thus motivate this publication. No effort to share the gospel of Christ with orthodox Hindus can hope to succeed unless the issues of

Tilak's life are forcefully addressed. These issues can certainly be addressed apart from the study of Tilak, but that so few have made even initial approaches on the lines Tilak laid out is an unspeakable tragedy that points to a need for his life and ministry to be more widely known. So his legacy lies unrealized, awaiting a new effort from a new generation of devotees (*bhaktas*) of Christ.

The utter fascination of Tilak's life for even a casual reader also motivates this study. The scholar cannot possibly ignore him, and the general reader will not want to. Tilak's grandson, A. D. Tilak, commented that "Tilak's was an exceptionally 'rich' life—rich in experience, rich in high thoughts and feelings, rich in idealistic acts."[1] All lovers of humanity will recognize here the marks of a *mahatma* (great soul).

Yet this will be no book of continual praise. Like most pioneers, Tilak had his weaknesses and blind spots. He left instructions that when his life story would be told it should be as it was, blemishes and all.[2] This study seeks to be faithful to that request. Tilak here speaks for himself as much as is possible from remaining records, so that this giant of the Christian faith can be met as intimately as is possible. Numerous points of interpretation and analysis are interspersed in the spirit of concern for effective communication of the message of Christ to Hindus which always motivated Tilak himself.

By his life and writings Tilak made a significant impact on the life of the Marathi people of western India in the early part of this century. His poems and hymns have been acclaimed by all, and it was through his literary work especially that he left his mark. Tilak had a deep interest and involvement in the social and political issues of his day, as this study will mention. Yet his overwhelming emphasis in both the Hindu and Christian phases of his life was on the realm of the spiritual and eternal. This analytical biography will also focus on the spiritual development and dynamic of Tilak's life.

Acknowledgments

Early biographies of N. V. Tilak were written by a missionary friend, Jack C. Winslow, and Tilak's widow, Lakshmibai. These are the foundation for this present study, and thanks are gratefully expressed to the trustees of the estate of Fr. Winslow and to Oxford University Press of India for permission to quote from these sources.[1]

Tilak wrote regularly for *Dnyanodaya*, the leading Christian magazine in western India, between 1895 and 1919. Much of great value was uncovered here. Thanks are due to the present publishers for permission to quote and to reprint an article as an appendix.

Various libraries and librarians generously assisted in locating *Dnyanodaya* and other sources. Especially the staff of the Day Missions Library at Yale Divinity School must be singled out, as well as the staff of the library at the Lancaster (Penn.) Bible College and the staff at Ahmadnagar College in India.

Little has been written recently on Tilak. An abridgment of Lakshmibai's study, entitled *From Brahma to Christ*, introduced him to some western readers. An Indian study, *The Experiential Response of N. V. Tilak* by P. S. Jacob, sheds little light on Tilak but contains a valuable collection of his translated poetry. Some articles have been appearing from

Mr. Malcolm Nazareth, and it is hoped that many more fruits of his valuable research might soon be made available.[2]

The generous help of Shri Ashok Devdatt Tilak is gratefully acknowledged. His contribution to the critical edition of Lakshmibai's account of her life with Tilak, consisting of introductions, footnotes, and appendices, has been invaluable. It is a tragedy that this brilliant piece of missiological research is locked in the Marathi language (*Sampurna Smrutichitre*, Mumbai: Popular Prakashan, 1989). Shri Tilak's unpublished paper on his grandfather, read in March of 1978 to the Church History Association of India, has been another helpful resource, as has *Agadi Step by Step*, his brief account of Lakshmibai Tilak's testimony drawn mainly from her account of her life with Tilak. The letters of N. V. Tilak were also made available by Shri A. D. Tilak. Permission to quote from these and from *Bhakti Niranjana*, the collection of English translations of Tilak's poetry, is appreciated.

Mr. Sunil Sardar of Yavatmal in Maharashtra, India, has done an indispensable service by providing translations from Tilak's writings. May God give him a double measure of the Spirit that was on Tilak! Mr. Pravin V. Thorat is thanked for 11th hour help in translating Tilak's Marathi letters. Mr. Malcolm Nazareth offered invaluable criticisms, suggestions and translations from his ongoing study of Tilak, to the great enrichment of this book. Presuppositions, interpretations and errors are of course the responsibility of the author alone.

Lastly, thanks to Professor Harvie M. Conn for kindly contributing a foreword.

Minor changes of spelling and corrections of grammar have been made in some of the quotations from the above sources to bring conformity and smoother reading.

Chapter 1

Introduction

Narayan Vaman Tilak is a central figure in one chapter of the complex and fascinating history of the encounter between Christianity and Hinduism.[1] Interreligious interaction is more widely and deeply studied today than at any time in previous history, yet unresolved questions abound and seem to multiply under deepening analysis. Narayan Vaman Tilak was not a scholarly theorist, yet in the existential encounters of his life he pioneered an understanding of and approach to both Hinduism and Christianity that commands respect and demands attention. Tilak's life as a Hindu makes an interesting study as he explored so many areas of Hinduism and decided that major reforms were essential. His life as a Christian became a relentless search for a more Indian expression of the Christian faith that would win his own Hindu people to faith in Jesus Christ.

In the area of Christian ministry among Hindus Tilak was a few generations ahead of his time. Like most such pioneers, his contribution in this vital area was largely forgotten by his immediate successors whom he so transcended. Tilak's poetical work and love for his nation made a deep impact and left a permanent mark on Marathi Christians. But his contribution to Christian work among Hindus made no lasting impact.

Hinduism has been radically transformed in reaction to Christianity and western education, and so also Christian attitudes to Hindus have changed dramatically. Never was there greater ferment in Hinduism nor in Christian approaches to Hindus than in N. V. Tilak's times. Tilak was brought to Christian faith by missionaries who were in the vanguard of new, positive approaches to Hinduism. Tilak followed in this line of fulfillment theology, deepening and applying what others had begun. He wrote,

> Christ came not to destroy but to fulfill, and his learned disciples have ever interpreted the literature of the world in a discerning and constructive way. Our task is not to condemn indiscriminately, but rather to appreciate the best that there is in persons, to hold up to them their own acknowledged best, and then to try lovingly to make that best of theirs still better.[2]

Traditional Missionary Approaches to Hinduism

The traditional missionary approach to Hinduism had been condemnatory toward virtually everything Hindu. Christian missionaries began arriving in India from 1500 when the Portuguese gained a foothold for their empire. Initially most missionaries saw only the superstitions of popular Hinduism, and the standard message was a blast against idolatry. Too often in the process of preaching Christ missionaries were involved in public ridicule of Hinduism. As deeper understanding of Hinduism developed, more sensitivity was shown. Yet almost up to the turn of the twentieth century the basic missionary assumption was that Hinduism is nothing but error and Christianity is nothing but truth.

The mission through which N. V. Tilak came to Christ was the American Marathi Mission, the first Protestant mission to western India. All missionary history in India is inextricably tied to colonialism, a stigma that mars the work of Christ in India to this day. The pioneers of the American Marathi Mission, Gordon Hall and Samuel and Roxana Nott, met considerable opposition to beginning their work in Bombay, and actually at one point fled from the city to avoid deportation to England. But their arrival in 1813 coincided with political changes in the British empire that finally made it possible for them to remain and freely begin Christian work among the Hindus.

The Protestant missionary strategy was always primarily translating the Bible. William Carey and his colleagues on the eastern side of India had already published a Marathi New Testament, but it was found to be a local dialect only and not suitable for wide use. By 1817 the new missionaries began printing their Marathi gospels, but literature was of little use among a largely illiterate people. Already in 1815 a school was opened, and "from then onwards much of the pioneers' time was spent in school work."[3]

In 1830 Alexander Duff arrived in Calcutta. Duff began the great work of Christian higher education, with support from elder statesman Carey. John Wilson followed his example in Bombay, where English medium higher education began in the early 1830s. John Wilson is best known for this work, but he was a deeply learned missionary who labored in Bombay for forty-six years. Disturbed by the general indifference to the Christian message, Wilson opted for a stronger approach.

"I thought on the days of Paul when he stood on Mars hill. ... I have consequently challenged Hindoos, Parsees and Mussulmans to the combat."[4] The combat was public debate and literary wars in which Wilson sought to expose

Hinduism as empty and fraudulent ("the grandest embodiment of Gentile error").[5] It was only gradually over many years that this combative, critical approach was seen to be ineffective in winning large numbers of Hindus to faith in Christ. The abandonment of this early approach (sadly, still not abandoned by all Christians) could not erase a legacy of deep resentment against the Christian message which remains to the present time.

Philosophical and Popular Expressions of Hinduism

With the beginning of the twentieth century new ideas were coming to dominate the missionary scene. The new thinking was influenced by the great advances being made in Indological studies, highlighted by the publication of the series *The Sacred Books of the East*, edited by F. Max Mueller.[6] As the riches of classical Hinduism and its philosophical schools became known, so also a deeper appreciation of popular Hinduism developed.

Philosophical Hinduism centers on expositions and developments of the Upanishads, the last section of the Vedic scriptures. While Hindus esteem all of the Vedic scriptures in theory, the reality is that Vedic gods and practices are almost completely forgotten by virtually all Hindus. The philosophical teachings of the Upanishads are summarized in a later scripture, the Bhagavad Gita, which is mainly responsible for any popular understanding of the higher philosophy.

Popular Hinduism looks for ancient authority to the massive epic works of the Ramayana and Mahabharata, of which the Bhagavad Gita is a small section, and to the Puranas. These are officially lesser (and definitely much later) scriptures than the Vedas but are the true foundation for living Hinduism. In the Christian era Buddhism was eradicated from India under the growth of this popular Hinduism.

Although it is rooted in the Sanskrit scriptures of the epics, and to a lesser extent the Bhagavad Gita, popular Hinduism grew and thrived on poetry composed in the various vernacular languages of India. Beginning in the seventh century in the southern Tamil country with the Nayanars and the Alvars a devotional (*bhakti*) movement focusing on God as a gracious personality spread to every area of India.

Around A.D. 1275 the first of the renowned Marathi *bhakti* poets, Dnyaneswara, was born. A series of other outstanding poets followed in the succeeding centuries, culminating in the great Tukaram, born in 1608. Missionaries of the American Marathi Mission had become students of the heart warming literature of Marathi *bhakti* and realized that much truth was present in this popular literature. Justin Abbott, a missionary deeply involved with Tilak, later translated and published a series of 12 volumes on the Hindu poet-saints of Maharashtra.[7]

This popular Hinduism is the true Hinduism of the people of India. The Hinduism of the philosophers (*jñanis*, those who follow the way of meditation and knowledge) usually seems to win its way into the books on Hinduism. But it is *bhakti*, the way of personal devotion to God, that has won the hearts of Hindus.[8]

The great themes of the *bhakti* poets ring so true to Christian teaching that there is much speculation on the possibility of Christian influence on them. There is no reason to conclude that these themes arose from outside Hinduism itself, however. Tukaram spoke fully within his Hindu tradition when he prayed to God in these words:

1. Thou art the giver of help to the helpless. Thou art the destroyer of the sorrows and the sinful temptations of the heart. I have now come to Thee as a

suppliant. Save me, O merciful One, my Mother and Father.

2. In the company of Thy saints give me the privilege of serving their feet, so that I may not forget Thee. This is the longing of my life. Fulfil this desire of my heart, O God!

3. Give me trust and love of Thee. Give me the love of singing the praise of Thy goodness and Thy name. Free me from the clutches of hindrances, and listen to my plea.

4. I have nothing more to ask of Thee, such as happiness, property, royalty and wealth. This will not place a burden on Thee, except that of the worship (I give Thee), O my Mother and Father.

5. Joining palm to palm (in prayer) I place my head at Thy feet. Tukaram is pleading, O Pandharinath. Inspire me with mirth and delight in Thy glorious exploits. Fulfil the longing of my heart, O my Mother and Father.[9]

Bhakti poetry is full of the sentiments expressed here. Tukaram addressed his prayer to God as manifested in the temple at Pandharpur (Pandharinath in the poem), a black stone idol that hardly impresses the outside observer. Yet still today the words of Tukaram are known and sung wherever the Marathi language is known. This is the Hinduism of the heart, not to be mocked but to be honored as one of the highest expressions of the human spirit.

Fulfillment Theology

In the light of this Hinduism, Justin Abbott and N. V. Tilak adhered to what is known today as the fulfillment school of thought. The greatest influence in popularizing this Christian approach to Hinduism was J. N. Farquhar of the YMCA. The manifesto of the movement is Farquhar's book, The Crown of Hinduism, in which he suggests that all that is deepest and truest in Hinduism comes to fulfillment in Jesus Christ. The last section of the last chapter of his massive and sensitive study is entitled "Christ the Crown of Hinduism."[10]

The fulfillment school was committed to sound scholarship in Hindu studies, but even more to a sympathetic understanding of Hindu thought and practices. A positive regard for the many admirable qualities of Hinduism was strongly affirmed as essential at the great missionary council at Edinburgh in 1910. The council concluded that "the missionary to Hindus should possess, and not merely assume, a *sympathetic attitude towards India's most ancient religion.*"[11] This marked a vast improvement over previous anti-Hindu rhetoric. The goal of the missionary enterprise had become the transformation rather than the destruction of Hindu teaching and life.

Hinduism was now being interpreted in a more positive light, yet the fulfillment school strongly asserted that the impressive ideals of Hinduism cannot be fully worked out within Hinduism itself. The Hindu esteem for the other-worldly figure, the man of renunciation who forgets himself in God-consciousness, finds no historical expression in Hinduism to match Jesus of Nazareth. The peace that is constantly sought and at different levels found in Hinduism is promised by Jesus Christ to all His disciples.[12] The longing for union with God which permeates all of Hinduism comes to experiential realization through the Spirit of Jesus Christ, by whom God comes to live within the human personality.[13]

The fulfillment school agreed with Hindu critics that there are many points of weakness and corruption in Christianity as a religious system. But the supremacy of Jesus Christ as Lord and Savior was resolutely upheld. The

Christian message should not be Christianity, most certainly not western civilization, but Jesus Christ. Obviously Jesus could not be brought into the Hindu world without change, yet as Farquhar pointed out it was constructive and not destructive change that Christ would bring:

> He does not come to destroy. To Him all that is great and good is dear, the noble art of India, the power and spirituality of its best literature, the beauty and simplicity of Hindu village life, the love and tenderness of the Hindu home, the devotion and endurance of the ascetic schools. ... True, Christ passes everything through His refiner's fire, in order that the dross, which Hindus know so well, may pass away; but the gold will then shine all the brighter.[14]

To fully analyze the strengths and weaknesses of the fulfillment school is beyond the scope of this chapter, but it is noted, as N. V. Tilak must be seen in the light of this thinking.[15] Probably Tilak's most quoted line is his claim that he "came to Christ over Tukaram's bridge."[16] His understanding of Tukaram prepared him for reception of the teaching and experience of Christ. Tilak is living proof of at least partial validity in the fulfillment school, and much of his life story will involve implicit analysis of this approach to Hinduism.

The fulfillment school never developed as its early proponents had hoped. J. Z. Hodge commented at the Tambaram International Missionary Conference in 1938 that "it is nothing less than a tragedy that the work begun so well by the late Dr. Farquhar has never been adequately followed up."[17] Some post-Vatican II Roman Catholic theorizing on Hinduism was largely a rebirth of this approach to Hindu-Christian relations. Protestants developed new ideas that largely ignored rather than refuted the fulfillment concept.

The dismissal of the view that Christ fulfills Hinduism, as insightfully pointed out by Eric Sharpe, "is to be seen far less in the progressive development of Christian theology, or in deepening insights into the nature, the beliefs and practices of Hinduism … than in the progressive disintegration of Christian theological thought."[18] It has become acceptable today to grant that God provides salvation through Hinduism and its myths and deities as freely as through Christ, a clear indication of the death of biblical theology. Farquhar (and Tilak) attempted to be serious in his understanding of Hinduism and yet faithful to biblical revelation. The fulfillment school remains the best attempt yet made to develop a model for biblical Christian witness among Hindus.

By naming Tilak along with J. N. Farquhar it must not be taken that he was a leader in the theory of fulfillment. His greatness was not in theorizing but in action. In fact, no one ever moved as radically as N. V. Tilak in applying the thought of fulfillment into action. His action was so decisive and profound that it must be considered far in advance of what the fulfillment school itself visualized.

The study of a man of action such as Tilak must never descend to mere historical or theoretical interest. Many practical points on Christian witness among Hindus will be developed and analyzed as Tilak's life story unfolds. The legacy of N. V. Tilak is to those who will step beyond accepted norms and pioneer into Hindu contexts with the life and message of Jesus.

When shall these longings be sufficed
   That stir my spirit night and day?
   When shall I see my country lay
Her homage at the Feet of Christ?

How thirst I for that blessed day
   When India's spiritual power
   And all her ancient wisdom's dower
Shall own His consummating sway.

(Christayana 2:64, 66)[19]

Chapter 2

Early Years

The best and the worst of Hinduism are seen in the early life of Narayan Vaman Tilak. He was born in late 1861 in what is today Maharashtra state in western India. He was a Brahmin, the highest among the Hindu caste groups. He was raised in his mother's family home and was molded by the atmosphere of that family.

Tilak wrote of his mother, Janakibai, "My mother, I do not know how, was a woman of faith and love. Though she never talked to us of Christ, yet she taught us to fear God, and to love all."[1] The deep personal devotion for God that marks so much of popular Hinduism was clearly evident in Janakibai and her father.

Janakibai's father was a sadhu devoted to God as Narayan (Vishnu). He had forsaken normal home life after a pilgrimage to Pandharpur, a center of popular *bhakti* Hinduism, and spent all his days in religious devotion. He changed young Tilak's name to Narayan and took him for walks in the woods, where he sang spiritual songs (*bhajans*) and chanted the sacred name of Narayan. In this way Tilak imbibed the *bhakti* spirit of popular Hinduism with its emphasis on God and his grace and the desperate human need to experience God.

Tilak's poetic instincts came from his mother, as did early encouragement to poetic endeavor. Love for both poetry and his mother was only increased by the distant and even hostile relationship between Tilak and his father, Wamanrao. Tilak's wife Lakshmibai said of Wamanrao, "His estimation of a person depended on goblins, sorcery, demon-possession, luck, planets, horoscopes, and the length and shape of fingers and toes."[2] Narayan was born under evil stars, and Wamanrao at that time lost his job. So Narayan was treated as a step-son. Once he was afflicted with guinea worms in his legs and Wamanrao told him it would be a great pleasure if he became lame.[3]

Wamanrao's favorite goddess would possess him every Friday. The only account of this occurred after Tilak's marriage, but it illustrates the rigid, superstitious faith of Wamanrao that so strikingly contrasts with Janakibai. Wamanrao would insist that the whole family be present for the coming of the goddess, who was worshipped by all when she made her presence known in him. Questions were asked and the goddess glibly answered. All the week's problems were resolved in this way. Lakshmibai writes of her terror at this performance, not lessened by the goddess accusing her of bringing bad luck on the home! Tilak counted that message worth nothing and refused to offer worship. Wamanrao was enraged at his son when told of this after the goddess had left him.

Wamanrao's long absences from home gave Narayan welcome freedom with his beloved mother. That young Tilak would help his mother with housework upset Wamanrao, but it was poetry that fired his temper most. Only two couplets of Janakibai's poetry survived the opposition of her husband, and disdain greeted Tilak's early efforts.

Janakibai could read and write, which were rare attainments for a woman of that time. She had two lady missionary friends who gave her the book of Proverbs, which she constantly read. When Wamanrao learned of this he burned the precious book. Narayan responded by throwing his father's tobacco accessories in a well. After a severe beating Tilak ran away from home and was gone for six months.

Taught by his mother, Tilak early became a devout reader. Even under his mother's tutelage he neglected mathematics for poetry. Then at just fourteen years of age, Tilak lost his saintly mother due to his father's harsh, hot-tempered ways. Ever the loyal, loving wife, Janakibai traveled forty miles on foot with two children in the hot season to see her husband who had sent word of his impending death and called her to come. But it was a ruse, testing Janakibai's faithfulness. Arriving to a fully healthy husband, Janakibai in joy began to serve, only to be abused and kicked when she asked Wamanrao for help with a water pot. Collapsing, she passed away eight days later, saying nothing but the name of Ram (Rama, an incarnation of Vishnu) until she died.

Beyond Parental Influence

His mother's death devastated Tilak. In loyalty to her he stayed by his father until the final rites for Janakibai were performed. He then left his father to begin his own life outside that oppressive influence. Surely Tilak's later revolt against orthodox Hinduism is not unrelated to the barren and superstitious orthodoxy of his father.

Without money, friends or sense of direction Tilak was led by the unseen hand of God into relationships with two men whose input shaped the whole of his life. He wandered to a nearby city and was first befriended by another young Brahmin and taken in by his widowed mother. There Tilak met the famed Vedic scholar Ganesh Shastri Lele. Lele saw Tilak's potential and trained him with a thorough Sanskrit education. Under Lele's guidance Tilak soon won first prize in an elocution and oratory competition. Tilak always said he had two gurus, his mother and Lele.

Tilak saw that the English language was increasingly necessary, so set himself to learn it by memorizing a dictionary! After Tilak reached the letter M, a headmaster took him in for free education. This lasted just over two years, as his father learned of Tilak's presence and sent his four remaining children (twelve had died after birth), along with some financial help, to be under Narayan's care.

Tilak's formal education ended under the pressure of family duties, yet this schoolmaster left his mark. "He made the little heads under his charge as dizzy with patriotism as his own," wrote Tilak later. "I well remember that even in my tender years, when I sat in the schoolroom for a lesson in geography, my mind was absent; for I was musing over the deep problem of India's future."[4]

No one would have dreamed that N. V. Tilak would come to see that India's future hope lay only in Christ. At this young age Christian books kindly given by missionaries were never read and often destroyed. Young Tilak opposed the missionaries with subtle arguments and silenced their learned sermons. This deep thinking, religious poet with Sanskrit learning and ardent patriotism clearly had the seed of greatness in him. Yet his burning passion for study and love of solitude in nature raised fears of eccentricity that moved family and friends to arrange his marriage. At eighteen Tilak was married to Lakshmibai, then only eleven years old. But marriage did not settle Tilak. His time of restless wandering was only beginning.

Father and Mother both Thou art,
  Whence may I fonder title seek?
  Yet even these are all too weak
To show the love that fills Thy heart.

Love which no man can name in word,
  Yet in experience all may prove —
  Steadfast, immortal, holy Love —
Such is Thy nature, Sovereign Lord.[5]

Chapter 3

Restless Wanderer

Marital life could not properly begin as Lakshmibai was still under age, and it would be ten years before anything like a normal family life was established. Narayan was constantly roaming for these first ten years after marriage.

Tilak's whereabouts during this period cannot be fully traced, but characteristic interests stand out. Much of his roaming was in spiritual/religious search, including at least one lengthy period as an ascetic; three times he began schools; poetry and oratory also raised some needed income; political involvement and nationalistic interests demanded his attention; and always his mind was restless for new ideas whether from people or books.

Tilak was barely twenty years of age when he began to wander the countryside as a *sadhu* (ascetic), apparently venturing as far as Dwarka and Delhi.[1] He ate bitter leaves, begged for other food, and eventually came under vows to another ascetic. Austerities during this time included hours sitting in a river reciting *mantras* (Vedic verses). During this period of nearly two years Tilak saw and firmly rejected much of Hinduism. Yet he knew that only a spiritual awakening could bring new life to people. The thought of a new religion began to develop in his mind.

Thinking that he would himself become the founder of a new religion, Tilak was determined to practice austerities until supernatural power was gained. It was commonly understood that by yoga the miraculous power necessary for establishing a new religion could be acquired, and it was only the approach of success itself that ended this quest for Tilak. He sat on a mountain top through all seasons and ate only what could be found growing at hand. Soon his life of hardship and constant contemplation came to the notice of the local people. Gradually pilgrims began to come for the blessing of an appearance with the holy man, and healings were reported in some cases. But Tilak was annoyed to notice that the focus was on himself only, his teaching counting for little. He saw that the pilgrims came only for worldly reasons, so abandoned his yogic practices, having gained neither personal peace nor a method of service to others.

Nearly ten years later Tilak again left home for an ascetic life. This time he was gone only a week because the vows would not be administered without his wife's approval. Even when not wandering off as an ascetic Tilak wandered from job to job, sometimes setting up home with Lakshmibai, sometimes leaving her alone or with relatives. Tilak's irresponsibility with money added to Lakshmibai's problems. His boundless generosity was to land him in frequent troubles all of his life from unscrupulous "friends." But that same giving spirit stirred compassionate and courageous action on behalf of the needy. He would feed and clothe the blind and lame and was enraged by exploitation of poor laborers. The schools he thrice started were characterized by deep love and loyalty for and from each student, again often to the neglect of Lakshmibai.

Poetic and Religious Development

Tilak always composed poetry in moments of inspiration. Poems and plays were written with astonishing rapidity when the mood was on him. Tilak clandestinely performed his work on the stage, fearing the displeasure of Lakshmibai's family. His father-in-law once attended a performance to investigate rumors he had heard. His rage at his son-in-law's involvement in theater melted away when he heard the beauty of Tilak's compositions, which moved audiences to tears.

Deep sadness came to Narayan and Lakshmibai in these years as their first two children died in infancy. The 1891 birth of Devdatt Narayan (Dattu), their only son to survive infancy, coincided with a job opportunity that led to some years of more stable family life. Tilak was hired to tutor the son of a wealthy man, but with the deeper intent of preparing for publication various religious treatises he had collected. Tilak took the opportunity to live in books for three years, studying day and night but failing ever to get a single volume through the press. He earned the title Pandit in learned debates from the Sanskrit scriptures and briefly edited a magazine dealing with philosophical and religious questions.

Tilak's fame grew in these years. He was continually winning prizes for oratory. He became a leader in the cow protection movement, writing a play that was published on that theme at great profit to the movement. His poems became part of a new birth in Marathi poetry, eventually leading to his recognition as the Wordsworth of Maharashtra.[2] But the religious unrest and resulting quest continued, finally necessitating the termination of these three happy years of study. Tilak himself wrote of that time, reflecting on his studies and conclusions and why the Bible had no place in them:

Finally ... I found a true patron. To this day I honour that
worthy man as my father. ... He had spent thousands of
rupees acquiring as much literature concerning the Hindu
religion, especially Vedic and spiritual literature, as was
available. For three years I was swimming in that ocean
of imagination and spiritual knowledge. I delighted in
study and I was given every opportunity by that good
friend. At last I prepared the philosophical foundations
for my new religion:

1. The Creator of the world is some particular, personal
   Spirit, and He regards all mankind as His children.

2. All scriptures are the work of men, and there is only
   one book giving a knowledge of God—that book is
   the world.

3. There is no such thing as former births or reincarna-
   tions. The sorrows and joys of man are dependent
   on a man's heredity, his own spirit, and his attitude
   towards his duty in society.

4. Faith in God and brotherhood of men on this earth
   is the essence of all religion.

5. There is no sin equal to idol worship.

In pursuit of the foundation of these ideas, I must have
become as abstracted as one of the ancient sages. I began
to study the lives of the founders of different religions.
With many of them I did not agree. However in Gautama
Buddha, I found one to my liking, and I thought of copy-
ing him except for his mistakes. The astonishing thing is
that not even into my dreams did the Bible or Christ enter,
the chief reason being the extremely simple language of
the Bible. It has become the very birthmark of a Brahmin
that he will only turn his mind to incomprehensible sub-
jects or those which will exercise his utmost intelligence. ...
I never met a Christian preacher, nor did any religious
book in Marathi fall into my hands, that could arouse my
interest. I had not even, like some other idol worshippers,
read one or two pages of the Bible. I had only heard and
read plenty of things against it.

I saw the Christians of my own country, but the unspiritual state of those I saw was deplorable. I used to think the only difference between Christians and idol worshippers was in their eating and drinking customs. These then were the causes that separated me from Christ and the Christian religion.[3]

As Tilak's five point foundation for a new religion indicates, belief in *karma*, reincarnation, caste and idol worship had been abandoned. He resigned his job on reaching these conclusions as it was not possible for him to continue to work for his patron and publish such unorthodox views. Uprooted again, unrest in life and soul began to wear heavily on Tilak. "There is in me no forgiveness, no peace, nothing; alas, alas, all my learning and thought are but vanity," he lamented at this time.[4] And to his diary he confided on May 21, 1894, "From now on, if ever the service of man be hindered by the rage that overcomes me then at that very instant, I shall put an end to this body."[5]

Tilak's sensitive nature made it impossible for him to be blind to or unconcerned about the hardships he brought on his wife and son by his incessant travels and preoccupation with study. Under mental anguish for himself and his family his health declined and for about a year he constantly found in himself evidences of serious ailments. But in God's providence the last stage of Tilak's restless wandering was at hand.

Spiritual Thirst   chorus: *Water, water bring!*

1. *Not by the well's water, not by the river's*
   Ease my suffering.   (*chorus*)
2. *Holy river after river*
   Weary my wandering.   (*chorus*)
3. *He who drinketh ne'er more thirsteth,*
   That living water bring.   (*chorus*)
4. *At the feet of Jesus only*
   Doth that water spring   (*chorus*)
5. *Life abundant, everlasting,*
   Christ is offering.   (*chorus*)[6]

Chapter 4

Conversion

On a short train journey to his new place of employment in 1893 Tilak happened to enter a compartment with a European. The momentous conversation which followed is recounted by Tilak himself:

> When I came to the carriage and looked in, a European was sitting there. I expected the usual experience of being turned out. Nothing of the sort happened, on the contrary, smiling a little, he made room for me.
>
> Here, O reader, with your permission, I will suggest one thing to you. Many European travelers and servants in trains become by their behaviour, positive mountains in the way of the spread of Christianity. The Hindu people have a laughable ignorance about the religion. All the same they have some conception of how a man called Christian should behave. Add to that the belief that every white man is a Christian, and Christianity is stained in their eyes by the vile behaviour of one Sahib. The trains and stations are filled with people who by their bullying manner deal deadly blows to the Kingdom of Christ. ...
>
> Our companion in the compartment was extremely polite and gentle, so much so that anyone seeing him would have been drawn towards him. I had with me

only one book to read, my well-beloved Bhavabhuti's *Uttara Rama Charita*. Of all Sanskrit poems I love best the noble works of this poet.

The two of us talked for a long time on poetry and poets. I was greatly pleased with the gentleman's conversation and quickly discovered that he knew a little Sanskrit, and was familiar with Sanskrit literature.

Slowly he turned the conversation, and then questioned me about my opinion of the Christian religion. I told him my idea of a new religion. When he heard of it he said with the greatest gravity, "I think that, counting from today, within two years time you will be a Christian." I was astounded at this. I felt his prophecy was nothing short of lunacy. We continued talking for a long time. The Sahib said to me, "Young man, God is drawing you. Study the Bible. Apply yourself wholeheartedly to the life of Christ, and in truth you will become a Christian."

Considering this an exceedingly rash speech, I cursed it in my heart. Lastly he prayed, took out a New Testament, and gave it to me. I disliked the book at sight; however, I promised to read it. I did not promise, thinking there would be any meaning in the book, but only for the sake of gratifying this good man. My station having been reached, we said an affectionate farewell, and I got out. It is a strange thing that to the end neither of us asked the other's name or dwelling place.[1]

Tilak kept his promise to read the Bible, which quickly began to influence his thinking. He began keeping a diary at this time so that his movement toward the Christian faith can be quite clearly chronicled.

On January 3, 1894, he wrote, "Within five or six years I shall give up my home, and set myself free for my country's service."[2] But on February 13, this:

I enjoy an intimate acquaintance not only with Milton [a European living nearby] but also with his wife. Discussed my views of Christianity and truth with Milton. Read him some of the poems from my diary. I am beginning to believe that Christianity is the only comforting, easily attained, happy religion for man on this earth. I do not believe that Jesus was the Son of God, but that he was the most generous of great spirits, I readily admit.[3]

Just a few days later, February 18, the steps toward Christ are remarkable:

My mind is being drawn toward the religion of Christ. Here appears a faith capable of giving the mind of man, peace, devotion, righteousness, salvation. Better to live in this small garden of Christianity, forever filled with flowers and fruits, than to inhabit the boundless spaces of Hinduism, with its thorns and trees, deep rivers, terrible mountains, fearful deserts and pleasing mango groves. Yet today I have not the courage to let such a sentence fall from my lips. Lakshmibai gets tired even of reading. I am held back only by fear of her, and love of her. O God! Guide her and guide me.[4]

The Bible and Prayer

Reflecting later on the momentous changes that came in his life, Tilak wrote,

According to my usual custom, I resolved to go through the book, marking with pencil the points worth noticing; but, when I reached the Sermon on the Mount, I could not tear myself away from those burning words of love and tenderness and truth. In these three chapters I found answers to the most abstruse problems of Hindu philosophy. It amazed me to see how here the most profound problems were completely solved. I went on eagerly reading to the last page of the Bible, that I might learn more of Christ.[5]

But more than intellectual study drew Tilak, as he also from this time experienced the reality of answered prayer.

One day I began to doubt the truth of Christ's saying, "Ask, and it shall be given unto you"; and like a rude, ignorant child, I resolved to put the words to the test. I prayed that I might get a book, then and there, throwing light on the history of Palestine and on the times when Jesus lived. I added in my prayer that, if my petitions were not granted, I would reject the doctrine that God hears and answers prayer. This was foolish, but God had pity on His child. Suddenly, the next day, I received orders transferring me to another office. To my great joy and astonishment I found in a box, under a heap of rags, three volumes, all religious books pertaining to Christ and Christianity, and containing information on the very points about which I had prayed. God continued after this to send me many wonderful answers to prayer.[6]

The time and energy Tilak was now pouring into Bible study could not go unnoticed. Quarrels with Lakshmibai and with friends developed, only to increase as Tilak began to correspond with Christians and receive books from them. "It was on the tenth of March, 1894, that I wrote my first letter to any Christian. This was to a man whom I knew by reputation as a writer. A few months after this date I believe I was a true Christian at heart."[7] A lengthy correspondence with the well known Christian leader Baba Padmanji followed, as with Justin Abbott and other Christians.

Baba Padmanji wrote of this,

Some days ago I received a letter from an unknown, learned Hindu scholar. He said that he had read my book called *Arunodaya* and others. Then he confessed that though he found in them neither beauty of expression nor any good quality if looked at from the point of view of the Shastras, still he was compelled to re-read them a hundred times. In them he found true sincerity, true worship, simplicity, and selflessness. He is reading my autobiography for the sixth time. ... This man asked for and I sent him many books.[8]

Hesitation and Surrender

By the middle of 1894 Tilak was committed to Christ, but in love for his people and for his reputation he consistently denied that he would ever become a Christian. Unable to endure disparaging comments about a missionary, Tilak wrote a poem on missionaries and their work and had it published under the name Jaganmitre (friend of the world) in the Christian periodical *Dnyanodaya*. The poem was easily recognized by his friends as his, and continued contributions to *Dnyanodaya* led them to conclude that in heart he was a Christian.

Above all else Tilak was held back from professing the Christian faith by his love for his wife. He had spoken to Lakshmibai about Christ, initially as if in fun. That such a *mahatma* or god existed could be easily grasped, but that one might renounce religion and family and friends for such a cause was beyond her understanding. She suggested, however, that lots be cast over the question. With prayer Tilak prepared three papers, the first indicating that he and Lakshmibai should become Christians. The second indicated they should not become Christians and the third that Tilak should become a Christian and his wife should follow him. Scattering the papers for their son to randomly choose, Tilak saw the third lot chosen three consecutive times.

But Tilak still wavered, and finally under extreme societal pressure, Lakshmibai turned back. Tilak later wrote,

> It is difficult for others to understand the persecution that must be endured, when his caste brothers find out that some high-caste Hindu has become a Christian. Though God may have been far from me at other times, in time of trouble He was near me, as a mother is near her child night and day when it is ill and crying. From all kinds of trouble He saved me. How many times and with how many men have I played hide-and-seek in most ignoble fear, but God did not abandon such a sinner.

I lost my work, I was reduced to an extremity of poverty; I had to go away leaving my only child. My wife with whom up till today I have lived as object and shadow, after great indecision at last clings to her own people; but God has not deserted me. In the end of November 1894 three nights running someone came and said to me in my sleep: "Follow Him. Do not be afraid." Then I could restrain myself no more; though there were so many difficulties in the way of my baptism, I was resolved to make it known at once to the world that I was a Christian, and thereupon requested Dr. J. E. Abbott of the American Board of Foreign Missions to publish this fact. He announced in *Dnyanodaya* and my greatest desire was fulfilled. Now ask no more. Did I not love my fellow countrymen I could easily let the world know what things happened next. But, no, it is better that they should be forgotten. May God be praised, I was soon after baptised on 10 February 1895 in Bombay, in the American Mission Church. The prophesy made two years earlier in the train by that stranger had come true.[9]

To Me to Live Is Christ

From Thee, Lord Christ, how can I flee?
What other refuge find but Thee?
Hell's fiery terrors on me roll,
If Thou be parted from my soul.

If Thou be hid, my Sun that art,
Night's gloom falls heavy on my heart;
Without Thy light to point the way,
All this world's paths but lead astray.

In sooth so vile and false am I,
Fears daunt me, if Thou be not nigh;
So crooked and perverse my soul,
No skill but Thine can make it whole.

O Saviour Christ, my soul's own Breath,
Without Thy presence life is death;
But, where that bliss to me is given,
I taste the very joys of heaven.[10]

Chapter 5

Confusion

Tilak never published details of the opposition he faced. He always considered that the radical reactions to his conversion came from a few fanatics and did not represent the real response of his Hindu fellow men. Playing up those elements could only breed further resentment, as seen in many similar cases right up to the present.

Further opposition to Tilak's conversion will be passed over here in deference to his own practice. It would, however, be serious negligence in a study of this kind to pass over the mistakes of Tilak himself and of his mentors in the painful and complex situations surrounding his conversion. Without implying that Tilak could have smoothly and without opposition turned to Christ, it can at least be concluded that the passage could have been easier.

The announcement of Tilak's conversion in *Dnyanodaya* was provocative rather than pacifying. "We are very sorry that our Hindu friends make it so hard for any of their number to follow their convictions," it stated. "Mr. Tilak will no doubt have to meet with still greater persecutions than he has yet borne. The usual slander and abuse will meet him in the public print."[1] That this proved to be the case does not mean it was wise to print. Tilak's own approach of silence and focusing on the response of better elements is the way to reconciliation and peace.

Lakshmibai's Misunderstanding and Anguish

When Tilak left home for Bombay to be baptized he did not even tell Lakshmibai where he was going, let alone why. Lakshmibai's record movingly relates over many pages the extreme anguish and despair to the point of death which she felt when Tilak's baptism became known. This heart-rending account must at least be read as a plea to Christians somehow to minimize the misunderstandings involved in conversions to Christianity from high caste Hinduism.

Tilak having run off as he did, how could there fail to be misunderstandings? Lakshmibai mentions some:

> Some distant relatives had told me that if I went to Tilak he would marry me off to someone else, and I should be compelled to do scavenger's work, and that I should have to cook meat. I was threatened with this and I had had experience of Tilak. Suppose I went to him, and he turned Mohammedan![2]

When news of his baptism was out, two of Lakshmibai's relatives went to Bombay to find Tilak and learn the truth. Tilak confirmed he was a Christian and asked that Lakshmibai be watched so she not commit suicide. Lakshmibai records their response:

> "Whether she lives or dies you have now nothing to do with her." So saying Keshav and Bala left, ... their hearts very heavy. As he left Keshav saw that the sacred lock of hair on Tilak's head had been cut, and he sobbed aloud. However angry he had tried to appear, his eyes had been brimming over from the beginning; now the very last tear was drained out of his heart.[3]

This expression of grief at the cutting of the tuft of hair at the back of Tilak's head raises the question of why that hair was cut at all. Surely Tilak did not need to prove the reality of his Christian commitment? Surely the kingdom of God is not meat and drink and tufts of hair but righteousness, peace and joy in the Holy Spirit? The great Tamil Christian poet H. A. Krishna-Pillai grew his sacred tuft until in his venerable old age it trailed most of the way down his back.[4] Here is one small area, but significant to Hindus, where offense could have been lessened.[5]

But Tilak's conduct to Lakshmibai calls for much stronger condemnation. Though his love for his wife cannot be doubted, Tilak's romantic description of his relationship with her quoted on page 24 cannot be blindly accepted. In the hard years of separation following Tilak's conversion a tragedy of errors was acted out by Tilak and his Christian friends.

Tilak clearly struggled deeply with the fact of this separation. On August 26, 1895, just over six months after his baptism, he recorded in his diary a deep longing and prayer of faith:

> At night a carriage passed by my door and I opened the window to look out and see if my wife had come. I waited so till one o'clock. O God, have mercy on this Thy lowly servant, on her Thy lowly handmaid and that innocent child. Bring us together for Thy glory. It is my belief that I shall receive the answer to my prayer this week.[6]

But the answer to that prayer waited four long years more.

Tilak wrote daily to Lakshmibai after his baptism, but often the letters were tactless if not cruel. Lakshmibai wrote,

> Every day Tilak's letters continued to come. They were full of anger, full of love, full of emotion. One time he would say "come at once," another time, "you have

no care for me. I shall marry someone else. Give me a divorce." He thought I should abandon all my relations to go to him.[7]

A Brief Reunion

Lakshmibai's health declined in the traumatic weeks following Tilak's baptism. Hearing of this he determined to meet her, and despite fears in Lakshmibai's family a brief meeting was arranged, but only after Tilak threatened to go to court. At great risk to his own status in the community Lakshmibai's brother-in-law welcomed Tilak into his home in Pandharpur, where Tilak's son Dattu did not recognize his father.

Tilak's behavior during this visit is hard to justify, but the emotional pressure on him was unbearably severe. What was intended as brief contact extended to a visit of two months as Tilak wanted to see Lakshmibai improve in health. He wrote to a missionary friend describing the situation:

> My wife is dangerously ill. Her position is quite pitiable. She is a noble woman burning with a pure true love and spirit of faithfulness. She promised on an oath that she would not break her caste to save her sister's husband when he took a strong fever at the news of my Baptism. She cannot and will not break that oath, nor is she able to forget me and be calm. My relations openly say that they would rather she be dead than joined with me. They ought to have been moved by this manifestation of woman's true love, but, instead, they are mean enough to taunt her the more for it. ... I have lost all appetite, and sleep, and strength, during only three days. I grieve for the native Christians. I love them and would have been of great use to them. Please remember me to all, and join your voice in prayer with mine. You know in what an unbearable fiery trial I have been placed, and you know perhaps all my circumstances. My wife suffers

actually from a broken heart. To leave her is to give a decisive blow to her physical life; to stay with her is to give a blow to my eternal life.[8]

Initially without but later with Tilak's knowledge elaborate arrangements were made for him to re-enter caste and be restored in Hindu society. Influential leaders of the Hindu community, including the later great nationalist and Bhagavad Gita commentator B. G. Tilak (a distant relative) and Tryambakshastri Khare, later to become Swami Yogeshvarananda Tirtha, Shankaracharya of Puri, contributed to these efforts. Lakshmibai surmises that he went along with the proceedings because her health had so markedly improved from the moment of seeing him again, and he did not want her to relapse. Tilak never pledged to go through with the purification ceremony, but only objected that so much money had to be spent, since he might recant.

But when no one could find a scripture text to fully justify Tilak's readmission to caste, he himself supplied one. On the other hand, Tilak refused to comply with the Brahmin council's decree that he fall at their feet in repentance, confessing his faults. Even this step was undertaken on Tilak's behalf by Tryambakshastri Khare; whether with or without Tilak's knowledge is now unknown.[9]

In the days before the final approval of Tilak's purification, cholera struck. Tilak excused himself for this reason, suggesting great scandal if he died in a Hindu home under the circumstances of his recent conversion. His true perception of matters was related to his missionary friend:

I am very much debilitated in constitution owing to the various anxieties to which I have been subject during the past two months. My wife is better, but I fear my leaving her may make her worse again. I do not know why I fear when I know everything is in the hands of God. I have at least clearly discovered that I am too weak to stay here, though human vanity shows me otherwise. The husband and father are still stronger in me than the devotee.[10]

So Tilak was provided means to return to Bombay until the cholera cleared and the final preparations for his re-admittance to caste were completed. All expected Tilak to return, but it was not to be. Soon, hearing that his son Dattu had been taken for a Hindu ceremony in fulfillment of a vow, Tilak sent a threat for his son to be sent to him or he would go to court. "Tilak had drawn his sword," wrote Lakshmibai, and this kind of shift in behavior can hardly be defended.[11]

Misguided Steps by Tilak and Friends

As the succeeding long years went past many Christians, unknown to Lakshmibai's family, began recommending remarriage for Tilak. Some went to the length of arranging his marriage without his agreement![12] This prospective bride died, however, and her sister being proposed as a replacement also died. This tragedy confirmed Tilak's resolve to wait for Lakshmibai and also provided him with a needed mother-counselor, the mother of the two girls. She above all others spoke up for Lakshmibai when Tilak's patience wore thin. Surely also Tilak's friends learned a sobering lesson about tampering with others' affairs!

It was Dr. Justin Abbott who clearly realized Lakshmi-bai's situation first and encouraged Tilak that she still loved him. He had Tilak study the Bible on Christian marriage and after praying with Tilak received his promise that he would wait for his wife. A warm and assuring letter reached Lakshmibai, promising to remain faithful and cause no sor-row. Sadly, the latter was not fully upheld, as furious letters followed again later. Once in a fit of rage Tilak sent a blank page, reducing Lakshmibai to tears and confusing all others.

Lakshmibai's story follows in the next chapter, but two final points of Christian insensitivity will be mentioned here in anticipation of her story. When she finally agreed to join Tilak it was made clear that she would not become a Christian. On the train for their departure Tilak provided fruit and sweets for Lakshmibai and Dattu but senselessly went off by himself to eat, as no orthodox Hindu ever would, in a Muslim restaurant.

Necessity rather than sensitivity had led to the arrangement of a Brahmin-owned home for Lakshmibai, so that she not be defiled. On arriving in her new home she found it furnished with all the wrong utensils. "In place of the usual brass plates and bowls," Lakshmibai wrote, "there were china cups, saucers, and plates; instead of our big, round spoons and ladles were knives, forks and spoons. I had never seen such things in my life before."[13]

Tilak made great efforts to de-Westernize the church, as will be seen later. Yet one of the most striking pictures available shows him in the western dress and collar of a clergyman. It is no wonder Hindus, including Lakshmibai, were confused; nor even a wonder that some reacted with violence.

I Have Called You Friends

One who is all unfit to count
As scholar in Thy school,
Thou of Thy love hast named a friend —
O kindness wonderful!

So weak am I, O gracious Lord,
So all unworthy Thee,
That e'en the dust upon Thy feet
Outweighs me utterly.

Thou dwellest in unshadowed light,
All sin and shame above —
That Thou shouldst bear our sin and shame
How can I tell such love?[14]

Chapter 6

Lakshmibai

In chronological order this chapter should relate only Lakshmibai's change of heart. But the story of this remarkable woman demands more than mere passing reference as part of Tilak's life. So Lakshmibai's early life and her own fascinating experience of meeting and following Christ will be briefly summarized.

Lakshmibai's family is in many ways reminiscent of Tilak's. Her grandfather had been hanged by the British government after the great uprising of 1857 because of false accusations by enemies. The shock of this permanently unsettled the mind of Lakshmi's father. He passed his remaining days in religious devotion of an extreme character, involving overwhelming fear of uncleanness from violation of ceremonial rituals. "Devotion" led to his refusal to interrupt his evening prayers to visit his wife on her deathbed. Fear of uncleanness led to special cleansings with water for anything and anyone in touch with the outside world.

Some twelve years after her father became "holy" Lakshmibai was born. Childhood memories are dominated by virtual slavery to the eccentric ways of her father, with bursts of light and freedom when he was not at hand. Even when neighboring Brahmins visited it was necessary to cleanse the house of their presence after departure. How much more ceremony was needed for contact with outside non-Brahmins! Wheat was to be washed by the bushel, a problem solved by washing only the top layer so as to pass inspection. For a time even salt was to be washed!

Lakshmibai's mother was also a poetess, and by dissembling as illustrated above managed to raise a somewhat normal family. She was even known to visit and cook in the homes of non-Brahmins, of course without her husband's knowledge. But a mother cannot arrange her daughter's marriage, and it was clear Lakshmibai's father was in another world and would not act on her behalf. So it was her uncle and brother-in-law who arranged her marriage to Tilak.

Most girls had their marriages arranged by the time they were four or five years old, so at eleven there was great concern for Lakshmibai's situation. Not only was the marriage arranged without her father's help, but his whims almost destroyed the proceedings. It was learned that the families of Lakshmibai and Tilak could not intermarry, a problem to be overcome by Lakshmi being legally adopted by her uncle. But father was nowhere to be found. An obscure verse of scripture was located giving a mother the right to hand over her daughter, and the adoption and wedding went through without further incident.

Tilak was a great catch for Lakshmibai since his reputation as a poet was already developing. Yet marital life for Lakshmi proved little better than for her mother and mother-in-law. Tilak's wandering life for the first ten years of their marriage has already been described. Often Lakshmibai was left with her very unsympathetic father-in-law. Money flowed through Tilak's hands without a care, leaving all the worry for Lakshmi!

Separation from Tilak

Tilak's conversion (baptism) was worse than death for Lakshmibai. For four months after hearing the news she descended to a state of imbecility, being cared for by her sister and brother-in-law. A number of times she made steps toward suicide. Only the loving concern of her family kept her through the first hard months. Letters and later visits from Tilak revived her hope and reason to live, despite the continuation of overwhelming pain and anxiety. Lakshmi's letters to Tilak were poetry only, as she had nothing really to communicate. Tilak was greatly pleased with this when finally convinced that it was indeed Lakshmi writing the poems.

The deep bonds of sacrificial love which bind together the extended families of Hindus are obviously seen in the care and concern shown for Lakshmibai. In her five years away from Tilak she stayed with three different families. Not everything was smooth, but she was always generously cared for.

That Lakshmibai might go live with Tilak again was never considered by anyone. The belief that he might force her to Christian faith or to cook meat or to do scavengers' work made the concept unthinkable. While her family sought to protect her from Tilak and his possible schemes, Lakshmibai gave herself to efforts to win his return. She wrote,

> I had nothing else to occupy my mind. Having risen in the morning, combed my hair and bathed I embarked on a fixed programme of [devotional] reading ... making offerings to the gods, telling my rosary and lastly a continuous repetition of the name of God. I ate only once in the day, and kept many a fast besides. All four Fridays, four Saturdays and four Tuesdays in the month were so observed. On Friday night I ate only rice and milk, on Saturday night a vegetable puff and on Tuesday night

I took nine handfuls of flour, six for the cow and three only for myself. The usual fasts ... were kept as a matter of course. All this was done as a propitiation to the gods in order that Tilak should come back into caste.[1]

Yet further, Lakshmi tried to force the hand of the god Maruti (Hanuman, the monkey god) by regular early morning visits to his temple. There she placed a stick in his hand with which he should chase Tilak home. She gradually pasted slips of paper with the name of Ram on his image, beginning at the head and moving down. She was sure her prayer would be answered before she pasted the name of Ram on Maruti's feet. Maruti's devotion to Ram was too great for him to let Ram's name be pasted to his feet! Instead of an answer to prayer, Lakshmibai nearly got a beating from townsfolk who lay in wait one morning to discover who was treating the god in this way. On realizing it was Lakshmi they gave their blessing to her cause.

Lakshmibai stayed in Pandharpur with her sister's husband and family for the first two years after Tilak left. She left there to stay with her brother's family when her brother-in-law relocated in Tilak's own city of Ahmednagar. It was considered too dangerous for her to be even in the same city where Tilak lived! While with her brother the sacred thread ceremony was performed for Dattu, Lakshmi's only son. No expense or trouble was spared as Dattu became one of the twice-born and entered his heritage by birth as a Brahmin. Tilak was informed of the ceremony but given a false date lest he try to disrupt the occasion. Tears instead of joy marked the three day event as Dattu was invested, the village priest taking the place of the absent father.[2]

Dattu's ill health finally forced a third move, back to Pandharpur to stay with Tilak's brother. Although warmly welcomed and well-treated at home, Lakshmibai was now out from under the protection of her sister's husband, who had held high rank in this orthodox city. The pressure of opposition and scorn soon proved unbearable. Lakshmibai decided to flee, with no destination in mind. Twelve hours before her departure Tilak arrived.

Tilak and his adopted mother had been praying together and decided that he should go to Lakshmibai without delay because she at long last would rejoin him. As he himself wrote,

> I had not the least intention of going to Pandharpur when I left Mahabaleshwar. While at Wai, one evening, after prayer, I was as possessed with the strongest impulse to go to Pandharpur. I came here; and, to my joy and astonishment found my wife fully decided to come over to me, with my son. In a moment I saw her defying all those relations and friends whom to the last hours she regarded with utmost faith and affection.[3]

Tilak's arrival changed all Lakshmi's plans. Now in June 1899 she would rejoin him, but there were still obstacles. An official close to Tilak's brother threatened to bring the law against Lakshmi if she tried to leave with Tilak. But this man was inexplicably transferred within two days of his threat. "My brother," wrote Tilak, "who was outwardly on my side, but secretly was rousing all the relations of my wife, utterly failed in his attempt."[4] Her sister-in-law counseled Lakshmi to join her husband, pointing out that Tilak was not requiring her conversion to Christianity. In the end this is what happened, and Lakshmi left to rejoin her husband with all but Tilak and Dattu in tears.

Changing Attitudes After Reunion

Arrangements had been made in Ahmednagar for Lakshmibai to continue to live completely as an orthodox Hindu. She lived separately from Tilak in a house owned by Brahmins and only Brahmin servants were hired to help her.

But misunderstanding and rumors ruined all the careful preparations.

Lakshmibai first went to her sister and brother-in-law with whom she had spent the first two years after Tilak's conversion. She was shattered at being ignored and rejected due to their disapproval of her even living as a neighbor to her renegade husband. Then her first house in Ahmednagar had to be vacated when the Brahmin owner learned of her Christian husband. In the second house Lakshmi was forbidden use of the lavatory in the compound, and later had all her servants quit. In her extremity of need Dr. R. A. Hume of the American Marathi Mission cleared everyone out of a mission compound and Lakshmi moved in.

It was a slow, gradual process that brought Lakshmibai to faith in Christ. For months she continued faithfully in the worship of her gods, but early on began also attending Tilak's prayer meetings. She was deeply struck by the spontaneous, personal prayers and worship offered to God through Christ. Caste prejudice was the insuperable obstacle in Lakshmi's life. Minor details of scruple had melted away because of the situation in which she had been forced to live, but personal purity from contamination was rigidly maintained. She was only cured of this by, in her words, "a sip of poison—nay nectar."[5]

The "poison" was water drawn from a well by a Muslim. During a summer vacation no Brahmin was at hand to draw water for Lakshmibai. Tilak felt it beneath his dignity to have his wife going to the well to draw her own water. Under constraint Lakshmi drank a mouthful of the "unclean" water, only to convulse into vomiting and a rising fever. Tilak relented and admitted his error, but on her sickbed Lakshmi was changed. She wrote,

> Lying on my bed I washed my pillow with my tears. Secretly in my heart of hearts I continued to cry, "Oh God!

What have I done today? Today what are my ancestors saying about me in heaven? What can I do to make amends for such a sin?" By not one or two but thousands of such thoughts was my mind overwhelmed. My eyes were tight shut at the time, yet all at once I felt as if a light was shining about me. I do not use the word "light was shining" as a form of speech. I truly experienced a brilliant light like that of the sun. My perturbation came to an end, and thoughts that had never before had entrance there began to whirl through my mind.

Tilak had received the answer to his prayer. All the chains of caste distinction, that had bound my mind so tightly, burst and fell rattling down. It happened in the twinkling of an eye. At that time the ideas that came to me were so clear, that even now I can reproduce them on paper almost as they were.

Did God create different castes, or man? If God, then would He not have made also differences in mankind? Birth and death, flesh and bones, intelligence, the power to judge good and evil, joy, sorrow, these things do not all men have in common? And if amongst men God made high and low castes, then why did that same God not also arrange an order of castes in the animal world? A Brahmin bull and a low caste Shudra bull, a Vaisya crow and an untouchable crow? Do such differences appear among birds and beasts? What is the difference between Brahmin and Shudra? A Shudra has no bull's horns protruding from his skull. A Brahmin is not born with the mark of his God-given greatness stamped on his forehead. If man and woman are of different castes, that's all. Enough, my caste distinctions were gone. From that day on I would hold all equal. The very roots of my caste pride had vanished. I would eat from anyone's hand, drink from anyone's cup.[6]

Lakshmibai soon proved the deep reality of her change by adopting two untouchable children who came to her begging on the train, and raising them as her own. But the radical break with caste distinctions did not mean the abandonment of her Hindu gods. At this point others could see what was happening to Lakshmibai more clearly than she could see herself. Regular attendance at Tilak's prayer meetings had brought her to fair familiarity with the Bible and its teaching. She enjoyed Christian worship and singing and praying. One Saturday evening service the breakthrough came.

At the prayer time, Bible verses were being recited by each one present. Lakshmibai quoted "God be merciful to me, a sinner," only to be challenged by Tilak. "God will never have mercy upon you," he said. "If being bound to me by promise, you desert me, what can I think of you? Even so if you live apart from Christ to whom you are devoted, how can God be pleased with such deception? How can He have mercy on you?"[7]

Tilak had discerned that Christ had won Lakshmi's heart even though she had not yet admitted as much to herself. On hearing this challenge, Lakshmibai immediately left the room and headed to the missionary's quarters, where she insisted on being baptized with her children on the very next day. July 8, 1900, Lakshmibai Tilak was baptized, like her husband refusing to receive the sacrament from a foreigner but rather by an Indian minister of the gospel.

Later Life with Tilak

For Tilak it was not enough that his wife profess faith in Christ, he was committed to her overall development. Not without setbacks and failures he succeeded in educating Lakshmibai and he developed her gifts for Christian ministry as well. From the middle of 1913 Lakshmibai struggled with bad health and this took its toll on Tilak as well. He wrote to his son in November of 1913 that

> I have come to be almost as weak and as sickly as mama;
> it is all owing to overwork and irregularities of life caused
> by sickness in the family and mama's inability to keep
> good servants. Then to add to all these troubles I have
> found myself a perfect pauper in brain-power, and I do
> not know how long I can work with pen! No one at home
> or abroad realizes what brain work means and I am given
> no relief by any one.

A letter from April of 1914 refers to Lakshmibai's "constant ill health," and a letter from July of 1916 says "she is very weak in body." In many ways Lakshmibai's greatness was not known until after Tilak's death, although the latter rejoiced in the positive reception given to her ministry during his own life.[8]

For nineteen years Lakshmibai served by Tilak's side, supporting him in all his radical ideas and changes of vision and approach. Then for seventeen more years after Tilak's death she faithfully served Christ.[9] She received honors from the Marathi literary world in 1933 and again in 1935. Today she is remembered and honored more than her husband by many in Maharashtra, and it is claimed by some that her faith in Christ was purely due to following her husband rather than resulting from deep convictions of her own.[10]

But Lakshmibai had herself refuted that charge:

> Some say that, pushed by my husband, I became a Christian. But they are deceitful. My husband gave me full
> freedom right from the start. After I became Christian,
> for 5 years I used to wear the *kunku* [red dot in the center
> of the forehead of a traditional Hindu woman, symbolizing her good-fortune being in wedlock]. This displeased
> my husband, but he did not ever say a word. About 3
> months ago I bade farewell to the *kunku* because a religious Christian *pandita* [learned woman] convinced me to
> do so. In brief, nobody pressurized me into becoming
> anybody or anything that I did not want to become. It

was through the effect upon my mind produced by the sacred experience of living in proximity to people who had become Christian from the castes which are considered to be low, that I became a Christian. At the present time, these people are not low, not devoid of intelligence. In point of fact they have become nice and tall, and persons of deep understanding. Besides, I have not seen religiosity in people of any other castes as much as in these people.[11]

Lakshmibai wrote songs and poems of her own, and finished Tilak's incomplete epic, *Christayana*. To Tilak she was "a gem unpolished" and "an angel."[12] Of herself she wrote,

Before I completed the *Christayana*, I asked myself, "What service have I rendered by becoming a Christian? My own spiritual uplift? My own good? And what besides that?" But when I started and finished the *Christayana*, this riddle was solved. I got the inspiration to become a Christian because I had this mission to complete. Now I think my conversion to Christianity is truly fruitful.[13]

J. C. Winslow gave an overly romantic summary of the ongoing influence of Lakshmibai on Tilak's life, yet in general it rings true:

It was she who was his first guide and counselor, the loyal sharer in his disappointments and difficulties, his aspirations and ideals, and the guiding star of his moral life, without whose steadfast encouragement not a little of his choicest work would have been left undone.[14]

Is there on earth a spot so fair
As can with that true home compare,
Where every thought of "mine" and "me"
Is swallowed up, nor shall you see
One speck of selfish coveting,
For Love is crowned eternal king?

(from Susila)[15]

Chapter 7

Christian Service

N. V. Tilak was a remarkably changed man after his conversion. The unrest that had worn out his body and spirit passed into a deep peace. On his brief visits to Lakshmibai all noticed the drastic improvement, Lakshmi even referring to it as his "exceedingly good health now."[1]

Tilak immediately began work with the American Marathi Mission, and remained in mission service for 21 years. His life centered around Ahmednagar, a city about 150 miles east of Bombay. Here he was initially both a student and a teacher at the mission seminary. His expert knowledge of Hinduism and Indian languages was always in demand for seminary courses, and with growth in the Christian faith his teaching developed into other areas as well.

Tilak was a leader and innovator from the start. His natural gifts and zeal for service could not be suppressed. It was not until August 31, 1904 that Tilak was ordained to the Christian ministry. By then his leadership stature was clearly established, and with little concern for the details of churchmanship he had begun to perform baptisms for those who requested him to do so. The church council, wisely refraining from rebuking Tilak's violation of church polity, rather affirmed his gifts and proceeded to ordain him.

The work and influence of Tilak cannot in any way be measured by recounting his offices and honors. "It is possible to say that the course of the thought of the Christian community was changed from the day of Tilak's baptism," commented Lakshmibai in echo of many others.[2] The commitment to serve humanity and burning patriotism that had marked Tilak's early life in no way diminished on his turn to Christianity. In these areas especially he made a lasting impact on the church of his day.

Service in Famine and Plague Times

None could fail to notice the formerly proud Brahmin and still-great scholar giving himself in service to the poor and needy. Already in 1896 Tilak put himself forward for service among orphans. The early years of the twentieth century were famine and plague years in western India, and nothing brought out the sterling character of Tilak and Lakshmibai more than their response to this massive human need.

At the height of a famine a problem in mission finances forced the closure of a boarding school and twenty-two young boys were put out on the streets.[3] The town was in an uproar of protest, but action was taken only by Tilak. The needy children were taken into his own home which already had five children: their own Dattu, Tara (an adopted daughter)[4] and three adopted beggar girls. For nine months the twenty-two boys lived as part of the family, Tilak and Lakshmi and Dattu having pledged to eat only what the others ate. The daughters were sent off to a boarding school, and though debts piled up there was always adequate food and water for all, until the mission could again take on the care of the boys.

Tilak's anger would frequently burn against the lack of generosity among his fellow Indian Christians, and even more so against the missionaries whom he saw as allowing and even encouraging this attitude. "To what a state of weakness have these missionaries reduced us," Tilak commented. "As if missionaries had a monopoly in helping others. Is anyone in need? Show them the missionary's bungalow. Done! That's all the help we Christian people can give. They have sown this habit."[5] His life spoke yet more strongly than his words.

When the plague struck, Tilak's adopted daughter Tara was afflicted and had to be moved to a quarantine camp. Conditions were horrendous, and initially only ten percent of those taken in survived. Lakshmibai and Narayan moved into the camp to care for little Tara. Tilak was busy with his writing, and sought God for the reason why they were there. Lakshmibai explained,

> He used to say, "Oh God, I do not as yet see why Thou hast brought this calamity upon us. I only know there must be some purpose of Thine in it. Give me the wisdom to understand Thy will. If Thou didst not have some plan, then why should not one of us have had plague rather than this little child?"[6]

One day an argument arose in the camp over milk. Tilak investigated and found blatant cheating of the poor and illiterate by those with more knowledge and authority. Tilak personally took oversight of the camp from that moment. Tara was near death for two weeks. Lakshmi cried to God in despair, pledging to stay and serve the camp if Tara lived. Tara amazingly recovered and Tilak and Lakshmi stayed on, convinced that God had led them to serve in the camp.

The camp sweepers decided to strike for higher wages, assuming that with their work so desperately needed their demands would soon be met. The first two days of the strike all the dirtiest work of the camp was done by the Tilaks. As they began removing corpses on the third day, the sweepers were overwhelmed with contrition and returned to work. Tilak responded by doing his utmost to gain their raise in pay, but berated their lack of humanity for such a response to a situation of great need.

It was not only crises that brought compassionate action. There was always opportunity for sacrificial service. Tilak firmly believed that the left hand should not know what the right was doing, so that often missionary colleagues and even Lakshmibai would not know of his generous giving to those in need. Once he sold his own property to get a fellow Christian out of debt. No doubt Tilak erred at times in his unsuspecting generosity, but how greatly this error is to be esteemed over its opposite![7]

Patriot and Poet

Tilak's ongoing ardent patriotism made the deepest impact. In Tilak's obituary in the leading Christian magazine in India, this tribute by B. K. Uzgare was quoted:

> The condition of the Christian community when Mr. Tilak was baptized was very different from today. At that time the whole tendency was towards adopting western dress and western customs. The language, too, had become, through the same influences, foreign in its style and, as used in the Christian churches, had become a subject of ridicule. ... The Christian community at that time was in a very unsatisfactory condition. It was neither Indian nor European, with no cohesion and no independence. The Christians were entirely dependent upon the mission and looked to them for everything. ... It was considered among non-Christians that to become a Christian meant to become a traitor to one's country, that to give up Hinduism meant to give up Hindustan. No praise is too

high to bestow on Mr. Tilak for what he has done by his
pen, by his speech and by his acts to remove this mis-
apprehension and to impress upon both Christians and
non-Christians that every member of the Indian Christian
Church is an Indian and that the Christian religion is itself
a great means of service to Mother India. Missionaries,
not being able to distinguish what was religious in
Hinduism and what was merely social, had taught the
Christians to reject every Hindu custom indiscriminately.
The result was that the history of the Christian church up
to that time was made up of contempt of the Hindus on
the part of the Christians and persecution of the Christians
on the part of the Hindus. Mr. Tilak saw that if this attitude continued, Christianity could never strike its roots
deep into the soil of India.[8]

The above quotation is perhaps extravagant in its praise,
as the issues of that time are still living issues. Were N. V.
Tilak with us today he would be distressed that so much
more progress still needs to be made in areas to which he
devoted so much energy. But progress was made, and
Hindus could not fail to notice the continued patriotism of
their former friend and coworker. It was this love of country,
along with his marvelous poetic gifts, that enabled Tilak to
regain quickly the love and respect of the Hindu community.

Tilak continued to write Marathi poetry, specializing in
family life and nature poems. He was a leading convener of
a meeting of poets called in 1907 to discuss the decline of
modern Marathi poetry. Tilak received one of highest honors
in the Marathi literary world in 1915, when in recognition of
his outstanding role among men of letters he was appointed
president of the convention of playwrights and actors. A
number of his obituaries commended his constant encouragement for young, developing poets.[9]

Contacts with Hindu society were never forged at the
expense of Christian witness, however. One Brahmin, espe-

cially scornful of the claim that Christian teaching surpassed Hindu, agreed to meet regularly with Tilak to study the Bhagavad Gita. The end result of this interaction was that Tilak baptized his former foe!

That Tilak could freely meet again with his Brahmin friends profoundly confirmed his patriotism, and convinced him that Christ also was welcome in India. Later in life he wrote,

> Thrice blessed is thy womb, my Motherland,
>> Whence mighty rishis, saints and sages sprang!
> A Christian I, yet here none taunteth me,
>> Nor buffeteth with angry questioning.
> I meet and greet them, and with love embrace;
>> None saith: "Thou dost pollute us by thy sin!"
> My guru they delight to venerate;
>> They say, "He is our brother and our kin."
> Let no man fancy that I idly prate;
>> Such kindness greets me always, everywhere.
> Saith *Dasa*, O thou peerless Mother mine!
>> Thy generous sons thy generous heart declare.[10]

Christian Writings

Tilak's greatest service to the Christian church was undoubtedly by his writing, and particularly his songs (*bhajans*) and hymns. His work accounts for 260 of the 798 hymns in the 1988 edition of the standard Marathi hymn book. The name of Tilak can never be forgotten as long as there are Marathi Christians singing praises to God.

The influence of Tilak's pen went far beyond his hymn-writing. Already in 1900 he started a magazine, *Christi*. The purpose, in his own words, was

> to meet the spiritual want of hundreds of new converts that are every year coming into the Christian fold. ... They

must be wisely fed with the milk of the word of God. ...
A paper which is nothing but spiritual and religious in
its character and tone. ... It will deal with 1) Christian life;
2) hints on Bible study; 3) lives of simple and devoted
Christians; 4) experiences of the Christian life; 5) suggestions about how to deal with different persons, etc.[11]

Another magazine, *The Christian Citizen*, was begun in
1904 and survived three years. Tilak was only the Marathi
editor, as others were heavily involved with him in this
bilingual publication. He also contributed regularly to a
Christian children's paper from his 1895 conversion until
the paper folded in 1909.

Tilak had his widest readership as a frequent contributor
to *Dnyanodaya*, of which he became Marathi editor in 1912.
Here especially he spoke freely on pressing issues of the day
as well as on spiritual matters. Tilak proved an effective
teacher of the church, although his primary gifts were in
other areas. His contributions in the area of Christian work
among Hindus will be considered separately in the following
chapters. His ongoing political interest and influence are
demonstrated by his dictating a political analysis just three
days before he died.[12]

The great literary work of Tilak's life was his epic poem
on the life of Christ, *Christayana*. The idea was brilliant,
and the portion that was completed is a classic of Marathi
Christian literature, but Tilak was never to complete this
work which he once called "the Summum Bonum of His
poetic gift to me."[13] Stresses at home due to Lakshmibai's
illnesses made it necessary for Tilak to get away to write,
but there were always other pressing demands and other
writing projects equally demanding his time. Only the first
section—eleven chapters dealing with the incarnation of
Christ—was written, and even that was incomplete. The
high, Sanskritized Marathi is far more difficult than Tilak's

other writing, but the majestic style and language are appropriate to the theme on which he wrote.

Even as death approached, Tilak spoke of the *Christayana* as a work God had given him that was not yet finished. He wrote to R. A. Hume in late January of 1919 saying, "I am sorry to confess that I have cruelly tried your patience and the patience of many friends, and am really repentant. From this moment I live or die for *Christayana*." But in fact a still higher calling than this literary work dominated the last months of Tilak's life.

Also during the last years of his life that could have been given for writing *Christayana*, Tilak was deeply involved with the writing of *abhangs*. Lakshmibai explains that "an *abhang* is a religious song or hymn written in the traditional metre used by the Indian Poet-saints, to express their devotion to God."[14] A wealth of *abhangs* flowed from Tilak over the last six years of his life. A distinctive mark of an *abhang* is the poet's signature in the last couplet. An example can be seen in the poem earlier in this chapter where Tilak, as his custom was, refers to himself as "*Dasa*" or servant.

Tilak's greatness as a writer is undoubtedly rooted in the early influence of his mother. His impulsive and emotional nature also lent itself to poetic expression. Pain played its role as well, as in his final illness thirty to thirty-five hymns were written. Lakshmibai pointed out that "the beauty of the hymns Tilak wrote increased in proportion to the pain he had to suffer."[15] Tilak's grandson, Ashok Devdatt Tilak, suggests that the five painful years of separation from Lakshmibai also served their purpose in enhancing the beauty of his writing and in raising his opinion of womanhood to heights unknown in Indian poetry.[16]

Tilak was well aware that he had an exceptional poetic gift. In a 1903 letter his frustration at Christian lack of understanding and appreciation of poetry is clearly manifest. He suggested that an occasion be arranged whereby he could spontaneously compose before Christian leaders in order to demonstrate his gift:

> In 1882 or 3, in Bombay in the Prarthana Samaj hall, I gave an extempore lecture in poetry. The subject was suggested on the spot. ... You are not to show any one that the proposal comes from me nor to show that my friends are simply doing this to display my abilities. If it is arranged write to Dr. Hume to relieve me and send me to Bombay for the lecture. This is not only for those stupid Ks [two Christian leaders] but [to] let the missionaries know what God given poetical gift means. The Hindus know it.

In the January 8, 1914 issue of *The Congregationalist*, an American Christian periodical, an article appeared on "The Tagore of Western India." Christian influence on Rabindranath Tagore was highlighted, followed by comments on the "distinctly Christian" poetry of Tilak. This information Tilak passed on to his son in a letter of March 5, and then he comments:

> My dear boy, it is between you & me. I tell you a secret. I am Tagore and much more. Pray that our Heavenly Father spare me, and after 2 or 3 years when I am free from pressing responsibilities, if then I shall have strength to fulfil a few of my literary plans, I shall live for centuries in the loving memory of my countrymen of the Maharashtra. But all for God's glory, & for his Kingdom.

J. C. Winslow comments aptly on this awareness of giftedness:

> He had an immense confidence in himself, a belief that God had given him unusual gifts and called him to do a work beyond the powers of most men. But he was alive to the dangers that this self-confidence brought with it, and was often wrestling with spiritual pride. He wrote

warning his son specially against the love of praise, to which he himself had yielded too much; and, if at times he seemed to regard himself with something of St. Paul's "confidence of boasting," he also shared to the full the apostle's utter self-humiliation in presence of the unmerited love of God who had called him to His service.[17]

Tilak and Missionaries

Tilak minced no words in his writing and speech when convinced a strong message was needed. He was not afraid to upbraid missionaries, yet never had serious problems with any, excepting one. Lakshmibai records some bold words: "To the missionaries he said, 'How long are you going to spoon-feed us? Let us stand on our own feet. Do not interfere. Let us try. Let us battle the waves; let us die, but let us learn to swim.'"[18]

Any theme that gripped him came to poetic description, and this missionary failing was no exception.

> You have set up for yourselves a kingdom of slaves;
>   do not call it a kingdom of God.
> We dance as puppets while you hold the strings;
>   how long shall this buffoonery endure?[19]

Frustration with the missionary system is one of the dominant themes of Tilak's life. It is important to note that in these criticisms Tilak was not reacting against missionaries personally, but rather against the system of western religion and denominations that disguised the true teachings of Jesus and the Bible. Missionary compassion and zeal, themselves good traits, contributed greatly to the crippling of the Indian church. Careful oversight of funds and of doctrinal teachings made missionaries into the "petty lords" that Tilak condemned. A letter to a friend marked "most confidential" dated September 23, 1903 says

I am really tired of Missions and Missionaries. These with their agents form an institution which is day by day degenerating. They are guided by selfish motives, they are slaves to self-sufficiency, pride and the world. Excepting those who join the flock and live in and for worldly motives, no other person can do anything for their country as long as they depend on these petty lords and their satellites. There is no end to their underhand dealings, there is no end to their dependence on their flatterers. I am educating my wife so that I may one day be free of this missionary-Christianity, missionary-injustice and serve my country and try to lead her to Jesus just as He guides me. Missionaries and mission-agents can never do more than what money can do.

An undated letter from late in life gives much the same opinion:

The great praiseworthy capacity of a missionary so over-awes an Indian Christian, and so limits him that under a missionary he can never grow beyond certain limits. Then some of them are the worst types of auto-crats & a few are certainly unChristian, almost Neros! Stupid, suspicious, jealous of their wretched kingdom which they call Kingdom of God, vindictive to the core of their hearts, pestilences in the vineyard of the Lord! But even such belong to the huge machine of a mission, and missions will let their good work go to wall rather than remove such wretches. This has made missions very good for *potbharu* [selfish idlers] and for hunters of money & honour who find the easiest way to gain these if they have the knack of deceiving these self-sufficient fathers & mothers of their own flatterers, forgiving a man who breaks all the ten commandments of God, but revenging one who breaks the least of their own commandments. With this opinion of missions in India I naturally do not want my wife or children to depend upon any mission if I die suddenly, and I know I shall pass away suddenly.

These strong criticisms must be balanced with other comments. Tilak's strong affection for numerous missionaries is often evident in his letters. His esteem for missionaries as a whole is evident in private communication to his son on November 30, 1914:

> I had gone to Bombay as one of the examiners of missionaries in Marathi & Sanskrit. How very painstaking and assiduous some of the missionaries are. It is one of the greatest trials to have to see any one of them fail in the exam because they all have studied hard; but one has to be just and ought to be just.

Tilak was anxious that his personal debt to missionaries be publicly known and recognized, to the point of giving instructions in his will that his picture was to be hung beside that of Dr. R. A. Hume with 'of him' written under his own and 'he took care' written under Hume's.[20] But no amount of personal gratitude or esteem could blind or silence him when he saw the gospel misrepresented within the mission system, and his life was a struggle to overcome this problem.

Prophet and Reformer

Tilak wrote and spoke as strongly and perhaps yet more frequently to his fellow Indian Christians:

> "Build a church with your own hands," he entreated. "Live on one meal a day, endure privation, but build your own church. How long are you going to drink water from another's hands? How much longer are you to remain like a cat with its nose in the dish? It is a century since you became Christian. Are you still to remain children only able to crawl? Were your forefathers thus? Are you not proud of them? Why do you bow your necks to others?"[21]

Exhorting on a more positive note he said,

> God so loved the world that He sent His only begotten Son into it. The Son so loved the world that He suffered

agonies to save His very enemies. Let the Indian Christians so love their own country that they will sacrifice all for it, and India will accept Christ.[22]

Perhaps only caste prejudice raised Tilak's ire more than this unnecessary dependence on foreigners. Once on a speaking tour in south India he was shocked to find high caste converts seated in the church building, while outcaste converts had to be seated outside. The next day, Tilak took up a position with the outcastes and forced the others to come outside with them to hear his message. He only continued his tour on being assured he would face no such prejudice again.

Reforms in Hinduism were raising the status of Indian women, but many still held the old orthodox view that women even of Brahmin families were only equal to Shudras. Tilak was a consistent spokesman for women's rights and dreamed of his own daughters joining those who were pioneering a new role for women. He began an annual Mother's Day festival in 1914 with the hope and expectation that it would one day be celebrated in all of India. This dream failed, but the practice continues among Christians in Maharashtra and that Tilak's writing made a significant contribution to changing attitudes to women cannot be doubted.

He composed many poems and articles esteeming women and their importance in the family and society. In hyperbolic prose he suggested that

> Ten schools could not be put on a par with a single educated mother. Before an educated wife, all learning in language is cancelled out. Before a single educated sister, all literature and music is in vain. It is on a single educated daughter that all future policies of a nation depend. But, of course, this is contingent on whether those people, who say that women's work should be next to the cooking stove, would believe all of this to be true![23]

N. V. Tilak's activities and influence were diverse, but the central focus throughout his Christian life was on his Hindu people and their need for Christ. His impact on his own generation was manifold. His primary legacy to future generations is undoubtedly in his pioneering involvement with Hindus. In tracing his growth in this area through the following chapters Tilak will be met at the deepest level.

The Lowest Room

Grant me to give to men what they desire,
And for my portion take what they do slight.
Grant me, Lord, a mind that doth aspire
To less than it may claim of proper right.
Rather, the lowest place, at all men's feet,
That do Thou graciously reserve for me.
This only bounty I would fain entreat,
That Thy Will, O my God, my will may be.
And yet one other boon must Thou bestow;
I name it not, saith Dasa, — for Thou dost know![24]

Chapter 8

Early Witness Among Hindus

Tilak began to speak to his Hindu people in defense of the Christian cause before he was baptized, writing anonymously for *Dnyanodaya*. He spoke regularly in defense of the missionary community in his early years as a Christian.

Missionaries were often accused of bribing Hindus into a change of religion, an accusation difficult to disprove. Twice in the year following his baptism Tilak wrote against this Hindu fabrication. He mocked a testimony of a Hindu who had once professed the Christian faith, received much loving charity from missionaries, and then renounced his faith and "exposed" the charity as bribes.[1]

Tilak wrote that many Hindus came to him asking for money to convert, but he always refused. He asked his readers to consider how many must go to the missionaries if so many came to him! Low figures of baptism were his final proof that only the sincere were accepted and stories of buying converts could not be true.[2]

This defense no doubt helped in minimizing the effects of damaging rumors, but it also started Tilak's interaction with his Hindu people on a critical and confrontational note. His intention was to make truth known, but he was exposing an embarrassment to the Hindu cause in these weak Hindus who would deny their faith for money.

Tilak was quickly embroiled in self-defense as well. It was axiomatic that conversion to Christianity meant the loss of patriotic spirit. Tilak was continually questioned and accused regarding his betrayal of his nation. His replies were rightly vehement against this ("death is preferable to losing love for my nation"), but sadly the vehemence also often spilled over into anti-Hindu rhetoric.[3]

Tilak's continual attacks on Hinduism in his early years as a Christian are painful to read. The missionaries influencing him were making sincere efforts to see Hinduism in a positive light, but they still felt it part of their duty to point out problems and weaknesses in Hindu thought and life. In his early Christian writings Tilak energetically followed this same approach.

A broad range of issues came under attack from Tilak's pen, nothing more often nor more strenuously than caste, which he called "the greatest curse of India."[4] Missionaries were already regularly writing against caste, and Tilak, who had renounced belief in caste long before his conversion, became a natural leader in the attack on this point.

"People have been enslaved for generations in Hinduism," he wrote. "There is political, social, and religious bondage in India due to caste." Still further, he asserted that there is no true love in Hinduism because of caste barriers.[5] The lack of cohesion and order in Hinduism, except for caste, was brutally mocked.[6] Tilak proved adept at winning arguments, but this approach has never proven effective in winning peoples' hearts, which is the primary goal.

Triumphalism

Tilak moved significantly away from these attacks on Hinduism in later years, and completely transcended this approach by the end of his life. He was less successful in overcoming a triumphalistic attitude. It seems that he, like so many other Hindu converts to Christianity, quickly forgot how deeply offensive it had been to hear Christians speak with a lofty air about the certain victory of their religion.

Tilak himself was held up as an example of the clear superiority of Christianity over Hinduism. He wrote to *Dnyanodaya* on October 8, 1896, telling of another Hindu leader who had come to faith in Christ. Hindus are often understandably offended by this parading of people who have rejected their faith. Tilak, like most Christians, was not sufficiently sensitive to this and so hurt rather than helped his cause.

Hindus considered that missionaries, united with a colonial government, desired at any cost to make India Christian. Tilak's rebuttal of the "at any cost" has already been noted, as converts would not be bought. Yet with more zeal than sensitivity Tilak wrote a broad challenge for Christians to evangelize and eventually bring all India under the flag of Jesus Christ. Published in *Dnyanodaya*, this could only be misunderstood.[7] Going still further, he asserted that "the Indian Christian Community must one day occupy the position of teachers to all India."[8]

Tilak was guilty of offending Hindus in most of the typically Christian ways, yet simultaneously managed to offend many Christians as well! He told Christians that

> Christian nations have thrown other nations into oppression. ... Even if Christian nations were not to let go of one span's width of land on the face of the earth, so long as in every home Christians are not found who return love for hatred, peace for anger and generosity for meanness, it is as good as daydreaming for us to hope that

Christ's flag of victory should be planted everywhere. Further, those persons who have been born in this country and who see the plight of their own country, yet their hearts do not bleed, from the perspective of the nation are enemies of their own country.[9]

Patriotism, especially when as fervent as Tilak's, was deeply distrusted by many Christians. As late as 1912 Tilak was accused of not being truly Christian because of his loyalty to "beloved Hindistan."[10] Some of his positive approaches to winning Hindus to Christ also aroused concern and even opposition from other Christians.

A new approach to winning Hindus was announced by Tilak within six weeks of his baptism, but sadly no details of his plan are available. He wanted to build on a Hindu foundation, yet described the "foundation" as darkness, error, pain and sin from which light, truth, happiness, and holiness can be truly seen. He asked for Christians to be patient, seeing his larger goal of winning Hindus to Christ, and expressed his willingness to be corrected if any errors were made.[11]

Christian Concerns in the Twentieth Century

In this first stage of his Christian life Tilak's positive emphases toward reaching Hindus echo the prevailing thought of his day. Churches and missions in India in the first half of the twentieth century were overwhelmingly concerned that leadership pass into Indian hands and that western denominational barriers be transcended by a united Indian church.

These laudable goals appear often in Tilak's early writings and remained matters of concern throughout his life. His first goal for churches in the year 1913 was that "all congregations become free, independent of foreign control."[12]

"We must be self-supporting," he said with the hyperbole of the times (or was it a serious expectation?), "and all India would come to Christ. All the foreign pastors also want to see this. There is no other way for us to grow, except self-support."[13]

Triumphalism was often happily married to the optimistic prospect of a church united under Indian leadership. At the centennial celebration of the American Marathi Mission Tilak's eloquence rose to great heights:

> The last century was justly the century of foreign missions; the next is ours; God Himself offers it to the Indian Christian Church. ... If we are standing on this stage of faith ... let us all unite and say to our God that the coming century is ours, the Church, Missions, our own country, all are ours. ... Once more then, in all humility, let us proclaim seven times that God Himself has given us the coming century and it is by all means ours, ours, ours, ours, ours, ours, decidedly ours.[14]

Tilak later concluded that the hope for reaching India lay in moving beyond the existing church rather than within it, and that latter insight rings far more true than the words quoted above. The massive energy expended for church union and Indian leadership finally produced the immediate objectives, but the dreams that these two steps would lead to Hindus coming to Christ have not materialized. The goals were good enough in themselves, but not in any way sufficient to powerfully influence Hindu society.[15]

Early Steps Toward New Approaches

Tilak's greatness is evident in his eventually moving beyond this perspective and modeling a new approach. The foundation for that later step was already being laid in other efforts to communicate Christ in a culturally acceptable way. Already in the 1860s Christian *kirtans* had been performed in western India, and Tilak followed in this mode of contextually presenting the message of Christ.

J. C. Winslow explains that

> The *kirtan* is a form of religious service, conducted by a single leader with a small choir assisting him, in which hymns in praise of God alternate with the spoken description of His doings when incarnate in human form. ... "A real *kirtan*," Tilak said, "ought to be a happy combination of music, poetry, eloquence, and humour, all contributing to drive home religious truth." Tilak himself was a master of this form of preaching, and men would sit spell-bound through long hours of the night whilst he told them the story of the life of Christ, and sang and even danced in an ecstasy of devotion to the clat of the castanets.[16]

The *kirtan* became increasingly popular for both evangelism and teaching under Tilak's influence, Lakshmibai along with many others learning the art.[17]

Tilak was never comfortable as an employee of a foreign mission. He made a few temporary breaks from the mission before his decisive final break. In January of 1904 he began to work as a volunteer, refusing the mission salary that he deserved. He explained his thoughts in a letter to a friend written January 3, 1904:

> I don't know whether in dream or while I was wide awake the Lord appeared to me and asked me to give up any dependence on man and depending on him he pressed me to go and preach the Gospel. My wife also had a vision which led her to offer me up altogether to God. I am, like Paul, now willing to weave my tents but with my pen and to earn as much as He helps me to do. ...
>
> I have also written to resign my connection with the church. All those who have faith like the apostles as regards their salvation form but one church of which Jesus is the head; and I now belong to all such persons, to the Church & not to this denomination or that. I believe I am allowed by the Spirit to go to any place of worship or

to any body of Christians & take part in their service but I cannot identify myself with any particular denomination.

At this time Tilak began a prototype of the later Christian ashrams by opening his home to any who wished to visit and learn. He wrote that "Enquirers from remote parts of India come and stay, and are helped to understand the meaning and necessity of the salvation offered by Christ."[18]

Hints were present that Tilak would break out into a more radical approach to Hindus. Already in 1899 he wrote that "there are not a few among us today who believe and interpret the Word of God in a Hindu way."[19] A year later he indicated a tentative willingness to drop the name "Christian": "If India follows Christ, accepts his doctrines and lives in him, let her temporarily call herself anything, if she thinks she can."[20]

A crisis was brewing in Tilak's life, and broke around 1904. His state of heart and mind are clearly expressed in a powerful challenge to prayer printed in *Dnyanodaya* on January 28, 1904. He wrote,

> Sons and daughters of India, who love Christ and love their own country, pray that God may raise up apostles in India for the advancement of His kingdom ... giving the land ... a long line of Christian Sadhus, of Christian Chaitanyas, of Christian Nanaks, of Christian Tukarams. ... Pray, ye sons and daughters of India; pray prayerfully, incessantly, earnestly, with faith in God and with readiness to accept what He offers."[21] (For the entire text see the appendix.)

The shakings that came in Tilak's life in later years were quite possibly in direct answer to the prayers stirred by this great call to prayer.

Tenderest Mother-Guru mine,
Saviour, where is love like Thine?[22]

Chapter 9

Finding Christ

A chapter on finding Christ certainly seems out of place at this point in the life of N. V. Tilak. But it was Tilak himself who considered that his true spiritual encounter with Christ occurred only after many years as a Christian. It might be concluded that his interpretation of his experience is wrong, but at least his own viewpoint must be faithfully recorded. And if Tilak misread his own experience an alternate reading must account for the cause of his error.

Tilak had been a deeply spiritual man even before his conversion. He had been a student of the Hindu scriptures and considered that only in a spiritual awakening could there be hope for India's future. Shortly after his conversion he began efforts to develop the spiritual stature of the Christian church, giving much attention to village communities.

The major focus of Tilak's ministry for the first few years of this century was villages in Ahmednagar district. Most of India's Christians have come from among the poor and outcaste of Hindu society, often in large numbers so that proper teaching and spiritual training were difficult if not impossible. The lack of proper teaching for these mass movement converts contributed to the generally weak state of the Indian church.[1] Tilak lent his talents and energy to building up these Christians and churches, initially part time but soon as a primary calling.

He was put in charge of village work in one area in 1904 when a missionary went on furlough. He continued on in ministry here for two years after the missionary returned. It was at this time that great changes came in Tilak's heart and life. It has already been noted how at the start of 1904 Tilak resigned from formal mission and church ties, so that his ongoing mission work was on a voluntary basis. One day when he was out walking he came across a group of pilgrims en route to Pandharpur. Tilak, deeply moved by their singing, from that moment began to write Christian songs with a much more deeply Hindu character. Both the style and the content, emphasizing warm personal devotion to God, had a decidedly Hindu flavor.[2]

Lakshmibai's further testimony to the changes in Tilak's life at this time must be recorded:

> Tilak used to say that he first became Christian intellectually, and not until some ten years later did he become Christian in spirit; it would not be wrong to say these were the days of his second conversion, and the disturbance of his spirit is reflected in his poems. His natural pride vanished to be replaced by a spirit of dependence on God. His eyes would fill with tears when he sang the following hymn written in 1906, and we to this day are touched when we hear it.
>
> > At last my Lord and King, to Thy dear feet I cling.
> > All lost this life of mine without the light of Thine.
> > I saw my own self stand the first at Christ's right hand,
> > In pride of strength and grace. Ah, now before Thy face,
> > That pride is low as dust. No more myself I trust.
> > Myself was my own foe, that would not let me know

How far I strayed from God, how dark the path I trod.
The name I bore was Thine. The will I served was mine.
I have no wisdom's light, no knowledge, power or
    might.
Oh Christ to Thee I bow: My all in all art Thou.[3]

Tilak himself, looking back to these years from 1915, analyzed his experience in this way:

I was intellectually converted at home in my own study room. Not so the spiritual conversion which took place years later in a quiet corner of the Mission bungalow at Satara under the spiritual influence of a Christian sister, Miss Hattie Bruce, now Mrs. Cooper. ... I wished to start work among my countrymen as soon as I was baptised. Whether it was serving Christ or serving my country I cannot say. After I started the work I soon found out that I was a spiritual dwarf and very often despaired. But God's dealings with me did not close with my baptism. A series of disciplines were ready for me. This prepared me for the service of Jesus by the time some seven or eight years, when I had the deep spiritual experience which is to me my real conversion. I began to serve Christ at the time of my baptism but it was rather serving my country than Christ. The sense of serving Christ dawned upon me after my conversion.[4]

It is distinctly possible that Tilak's interpretation of his experience is correct. He had set out to found a new religion, but had discovered that Christianity covered the points of his deepest concern. He undoubtedly carried in his mind the typical Hindu understanding of conversion as a change of religious communal affiliation. The great reformer Pandita Ramabai, who lived at this same time, seems clearly to have outwardly converted from the Hindu to the Christian religion, only to be spiritually changed many years later.[5] This is a danger to be carefully guarded against when Christ is brought into the Hindu context.

Against the "Second Conversion" Thesis

But it is hard to believe that this is an accurate assessment of Tilak. His deep, sacrificial service for humanity and concern for the deepening of the spiritual life of the church are clearly seen. That self-centeredness slipped into this and needed to be crucified, as the poem above affirms, does not prove that true spirituality was completely missing. On record are words which Tilak wrote before this "second conversion" that seem to clearly demonstrate the spiritual reality of his first conversion. Just eleven months after his conversion Tilak wrote these words about a theoretical spiritual seeker:

> He is not yet worthy to understand the Son of God. The crucified he knows, but to comprehend the risen Lord is beyond him. The best way to bring conviction to such a seeker is to pray with him. Through the great golden door of prayer he should repeatedly be brought into the presence of the Father, and in his heart should be awakened a true love of the merciful Father of this world. In this way he will come to know the Father and his doubts about the miracles will be removed naturally. I have always thought that God Himself resolves such difficult questions for the true seeker.[6]

Such astute spiritual insight seems impossible to reconcile with a purely intellectual faith. Other writings even more clearly indicate the place that personal devotion to and fellowship with the risen Christ had from the days of his first conversion. Referring to that time he wrote,

> As a Hindu I had, and still have, a typical respect and love to my guru; and, when Jesus became my Guru, naturally I regarded and loved Him with all the fervour and intensity of a real disciple. I experienced a peculiar fellowship with Him. This much I know, that I could not be happy if I missed Him. The following hymn was written by me in this period:

My Friend, Life of my life,
My Jesus, where art Thou gone?
Come quickly! I die for Thee!
The world around me is darkness!
Without Thee no hunger, no food; no thirst, no water!
Thy absence sets me on the rack of pain!
A sinner, miserable sinner as I am, —
Oh Thou, the Friend of sinners, Thou my only Friend,
Art Thou forsaking me?[7]

These words do not reflect a merely intellectual commitment. Tilak was surely wrong in his understanding of his first and second conversions. The fact that another deeply significant spiritual change came still later in his life also suggests that another interpretation of this "second conversion" should be sought. J. C. Winslow's impressive biography of Tilak makes no mention of this second conversion, implying that Winslow also discounted Tilak's interpretation of this experience.

At one level, this "second conversion" can be seen as a definite deepening of the spiritual insight and love for Christ which had been present to a lesser degree since Tilak's conversion. This does not in any sense lessen the significance of the change in his life. Rather this strikingly reminds us that radical growth in love for Christ and death to self is an essential aspect of life in discipleship to Christ.

There are, however, clear hints of other emotional roots to this crisis. Tilak's concern for the Indianization or contextualization of Christianity have been noted, but his insights in this area were still quite limited. Tilak only came to his deepest clarity of insight and action in the last two years of his life. This "second conversion," however, was a major step toward that final insight. This was a definite deepening of the Indianization of the Christian message in Tilak's own heart and mind.

Though often writing on contextualization themes, up to this point Tilak had largely followed the lead of others. His original contributions all follow after this experience. As seen above, Tilak's view of his change focused on a spiritual experience he could trace to a session in a mission bungalow. Lakshmibai, as also referred to above, points to the simultaneous change to a more deeply Indian poetic and musical expression of devotion to Christ. This latter change probably impacted Tilak more deeply than he himself was aware of.

Christ-Bhakti

It is at this point in his life that Tilak moved into a true Christ-*bhakti* (devotion). This clearly released emotional resources within the depths of his being. The exuberant spiritual freedom of Hindu *bhakti*, a tradition from which Tilak had drunk from his earliest years, had been bottled up under the western forms that predominated in his Christian life up to this point. What had been theory on Indianizing the gospel now in a more radical way was practiced in his own worship and service. The sense of freedom and life he experienced could only be interpreted as a new conversion.[8]

A deeper experience with Christ wedded with deeper steps into an Indian expression of Christianity were to Tilak his true conversion. From this time on, Christ becomes central and Christianity as a religion becomes secondary. "Pack up all your doctrines," he said, "and let us first find Christ."[9] It was at this time that he began writing the *abhangs* described in chapter 7, following the poetic pattern and using the musical style of Tukaram and other Hindu saints.

The influence of the Hindu *bhakti* tradition led Tilak to break out of traditional Christian worship styles into more contextual approaches. With cuttingly effective irony he asked what kind of *bhakti* it was that began on the hour when bells were rung and ended as punctually again an hour later. In the true tradition of *bhakti* devotion Tilak's prayer meetings would go on for hours with exuberant singing and dance. Yet Tilak avoided the human-centeredness of much *bhakti* emphasis, acknowledging that a person cannot seek and find God, but rather it is God who seeks and finds and keeps the *bhakta* (devotee).

The greatest longing of the Hindu *bhakti* poets was for union with God. Tilak not only used the poetic form and music of the Hindu *bhaktas* but developed this most cherished theme as well. Union with Christ is strongly and movingly expounded in numerous of his poems and hymns. Devotion to the feet of Christ and satisfying enjoyment of God in Christ are constantly emphasized, but above and beyond comes experiential union with Christ. The riches of Tilak's writings in this area make selection a difficult process. The last stanza of a popular hymn reads:

> Take Thou this body, O my Christ,
>   Dwell as its soul within;
> To be an instant separate
>   I count a deadly sin.[10]

Exclusively on the positive side of union with Christ, this poem:

> *Christ and I*
>
> As lyre and the musician,
> As thought and spoken word,
> As rose and fragrant odours,
> As flute and breath accord;
> So deep the bond that binds me
> To Christ my Lord.
>
> As mother and her baby,
> As traveller lost and guide,
> As oil and flickering lamp-flame,
> Are each to each allied;
> Life of my life, Christ bindeth
> Me to His side.

As lake and streaming rainfall,
As fish and water clear,
As sun and gladdening dayspring
In union close appear;
So Christ and I are holden
In bonds how dear![11]

The doctrine of union with Christ has occasionally been expounded in Western Christendom, but has rarely been celebrated in song or esteemed in experience.[12] Tilak from his Hindu background brings to clear focus a neglected biblical truth. He clearly speaks from the viewpoint of *bhakti*, which easily aligns with biblical Christianity. Often, however, his terminology borrows from other aspects of philosophical Hinduism, as in the epic *Christayana*:

Let me not dream I dwell apart
    Here on this earth and Thou on high;
    Teach me to know that Thou art nigh,
The gracious Tenant of my heart.

———

Grant, Lord, the prayer that I present:
    Whate'er there be of self in me,
    Let all be swallowed up in Thee,
Two persons in one spirit blent.

———

And surely he, to whom is given
    Wholly with Christ one soul to be
    Hath taste of all felicity
And unto him this earth is heaven.

———

Christ be my Brother and my Friend,
    Guru and King, my Soul, my Life;
    Betwixt us may no breath of strife
Find place, all sense of difference end.

———

Poison and nectar, pain and bliss,
    In the world's cup commingled are;
    But oh! than nectar sweeter far
The sweetness of Thy presence is![13]

The riches of philosophical Hinduism, with vital aspects of truth in the *advaita* (non-dualist) or monist tradition, are here applied to Christian experience. There is a reinterpretation and transformation of the Hindu philosophical heritage in the light of experience in Christ. To both the Christian and the Hindu, to both east and west, Tilak called for Christ to be central, for all else to be secondary beside knowing, loving, serving, and experiencing union with Him. Were this his only legacy, it would be enough.

Spiritual Craving

The more I attain to Thee, so much the more do I desire Thee.
Such is the state of my heart, O Lord.
I have seen Thee with mine eyes,
Yet still my eyes hunger for Thee.
I have embraced Thee, and should now unclasp my hands,
Yet still I long again to hold Thee fast.
Thou dwellest in my heart,
Yet still my soul burns with wild desire for Thee.
The Servant says — Ah! dearest Lord Jesu Christ.
Tell me, what can I do?[14]

Chapter 10

The Indian Heritage

Tilak's greatest emphasis throughout his Christian ministry was on the privilege it is to be an *Indian* disciple of Jesus Christ. It follows from this that western forms must be removed and indigenous Indian patterns followed. Tilak's emphasis on indigenous communication has already been noted but bears repetition here. As Lakshmibai summarized,

> He was convinced that by *bhajan*, *kirtan*, and *purana* he could completely wipe off the alienness of the Christian religion. He says of *Abhanganjali*, "I have always pointed it out to all my Christian brothers and sisters how much importance *bhajan*, *kirtan*, *pravachan*, and *purana* have in this country in religious practice and evangelism. We are really happy and we are grateful to the Lord that from the instant when Rev. Pulhari Wilson first started *bhajan* only within 7 or 8 years there are so many *bhajan* societies among Maharashtrian Christian people. Because of them devotion in Christian people is more and more increasing."[1]

Rituals and ceremonies need thorough change as well. Tilak broke with the normal Indian Christian pattern of a westernized wedding ceremony when his son Devdatt was married. The traditional seven steps of the Hindu ceremony were incorporated into a new ceremony with deeply biblical content.[2]

External rituals are more easily Indianized than thought patterns. Tilak made steps in this deeper conceptual area as well. He was primarily a poet and an activist, so no fully developed theology of Christianity in relationship to Hinduism can be expected from him. Most of his thinking in this area reflects the prevailing Protestant opinion of his time, yet Tilak's giftedness and background grant a unique perspective to his thought. Broad principles which were worked out in evangelistic contact with Hindus can be gleaned from his writings.

Clearly the greatest need of the Indian Christian, after a thorough grasp of biblical essentials, must be to gain a deep and true understanding of the scriptures and traditions of his country. Tilak brought this deep acquaintance with Hindu thought with him to the Christian faith. He exhorted others to work until they acquired a similar proficiency.

The Complexity of Indian Theology

The greatest difficulty in developing an Indian Christian theology (theology in the Hindu context using Hindu terms) is the vast complexity of Hinduism with its various schools of thought. Tilak exhorted Christians to avoid the classic Hindu debate about *advaita*, since siding with any particular school of thought would only alienate the others.[3] Similarly, he avoided a challenge that he was a *vedantin* by saying there are too many possible meanings to the term, and he could not answer the accusation unless he knew clearly in what sense the word was used.[4]

The terminological problem regarding *Hindu* and *Hindustan* could not be avoided. Tilak introduced a new terminology, suggesting that "a Christian man is a *Hindi*, but not a

Hindu."[5] Following this he spoke almost always of *Hindistan* rather than *Hindustan* ("land of Hindus," a commonly used name for India). There was little chance that this new terminology would become widely accepted. Tilak would have done better to take the more radical step of defining *Hindu* according to the original meaning as used by the Persians of "people beyond the Indus River."[6] But this would surely have raised a storm of controversy among Christians, as well as causing some misunderstandings among Hindus.

Once Tilak spoke more directly to this issue. A letter to *Dnyanodaya* suggested that all lovers of India are Hindus. Tilak replied that he was happy to agree if all others did, but expressed his longing for the day when even 1% of India will believe and act in this way.[7] Rather than introduce a new terminology, Tilak should have put his effort into strengthening this interpretation of Hindu, and boldly affirmed himself a born Hindu who would die a Hindu *bhakta* of Jesus Christ.[8]

Other examples could be given of Tilak's refusal to wed Christian thought to a particular Hindu school.[9] This is a wise procedure in evangelism, but will not be possible when a positive theology is developed. Relevant and practical theology will only develop in a worshipping community, however, and the absence of the body of Christ in a deeply Hindu context makes large efforts at contextual theology premature and artificial. Tilak's intensely practical mind set prevented him from wasting effort on developing a full theology when the overwhelming need was for evangelism.

Yet evangelistic approaches to Hindus must assume and influence theology. Tilak's practical interactions with Hindus and challenging exhortations to Christians indicate clearly his basic theological approach. His starting point is always a hearty esteem for the Hindu scriptures. A late *abhang* indicates this positive approach and pours contempt on efforts to import a foreign Christianity:

> Think not of India as of a child's buffoonery
> or a jester's tricks and airs;
> Here have sprung mighty heroes of faith,
> at whom the world trembles.
> Here have sprung sages that were lords of yoga,
> whose light abides unto this day,
> Men whose faith was their very life, their all,
> and the world their home.
> Yes, even here such kingly saints were born,
> and in the hearts of all men they shone resplendent.
> What boots it to bring here a masquerade
> of strange disguises and of foreign airs?
> All that you gain you'll squander in the end,
> and about your neck ignominy shall lay her garland.
> Saith *Dasa*, Here be the Lord Jesus Christ set up on high—
> that is our need alway![10]

Reflections in Christ on Hinduism and Its Saints

The practical meaning of this is worked out in a number of articles discussing Puranic myths. Tilak draws a comparison of Greek and Hindu mythology. Both were originally related to the worship of various gods, but Greek mythology eventually lost this, largely under Christian influence. Christians, however, preserved Greek myths and even were willing to learn from them. The beauty and wisdom of Greek mythology have appeal in all nations because of Christians spreading their influence!

In the same way Indian Christians should relate to Hindu mythology. There should be no destructive criticism but rather a search for beauty and truth. The whole world will appreciate the Puranas when this wonderful treasure chest of wisdom and truth is properly opened.[11] Tilak illustrated the practical outworking of this positive approach in evangelism:

> A Hindu friend, who was a staunch devotee of the god Dattatraya, once had a quiet talk with me on the subject of his worship. Afterwards he confessed to me that he had expected that I, as a preacher of Christianity, would naturally be hard upon him and upon his favourite deity. As a matter of fact I had begun with him by tracing the history of Datta and Atri from the time of the Vedas, and I had tried to show the man how the myth had gone on unethically until in the later Puranas it was made the basis of a debased form of worship. He seemed to be much impressed. ... Later I had opportunity to explain to him his own Hinduism, which, I said to him, had been to me a kind of Old Testament through which I had been led to the New Testament of the Lord Jesus. This man is not yet a baptised Christian; but I hope and believe that he will accept the Lord Jesus as his Saviour if only, while he is reading his own books, I and he can keep the Lord Jesus at his side.[12]

The Hindu scriptures as "a kind of Old Testament" indicates Tilak's belief that Hinduism contains a *praeparatio evangelica*, a preparation for the gospel message to be received by Hindus. His strongest emphasis was on the Marathi poet-saints whose style of worship and writing he followed. These Hindu writers not only lead to Jesus, but also teach valuable lessons to the disciple of Christ.

Tilak shared an example of how understanding Hinduism had helped his Christian understanding:

> Since I am an Indian, it is natural that I should take pride in our Indian literature and in our Indian *mahatmas*. But do not suppose it is simply out of pride that I sing their praises. Tukaram and Dnyaneswara were once my gurus; and, even though I am not now their disciple, I give them grateful honour as my gurus of former days. The tradi-

tional way of union with the Supreme through *bhakti*, which Hindu mystics have conceived and Hindu devotees experienced, may be summed up in the four words, *samipata* (nearness), *salokata* (association), *sarupata* (likeness), and *sayujyta* ("yokedness" or union); this has helped me to enter into the meaning of that series of Christ's sayings—"Come after Me," "Take My yoke upon you," "Become like unto Me," "Abide in Me."[13]

Tilak's teaching in these areas is undoubtedly true and needs to be more deeply understood and assimilated by the Indian Christian church. These concepts lead on to the difficult issue of the standing before God of these Hindu saints. Tilak cannot be commended as a fully reliable guide in this area.

Tilak wrote in 1900,

Nothing but the religion of Jesus ... can enable our beloved India to understand what God's idea of sin is, nor reclaim the sinner, nor regenerate the degenerate, nor make him perfect as his Father in heaven is perfect.[14]

This sounds like the traditional Christian teaching that outside of faith in Christ there is no salvation.

This traditional view is explicitly repudiated in a later article, however. He points out the error of Jewish exclusivism, indicates the difficult status of Ephesian semi-Christians in Acts 19, and points out how Enoch, Noah, Abraham and many others were taken to heaven despite not knowing the law of Moses nor the grace taught by Paul. He believes God will be just in His judgments and will not condemn people for not acting on what they do not know.

Tilak goes a step further still in affirming that he does not think all his ancestors will be in hell. He expresses pity for those who think this way. His only illustration of a Hindu who would not go to hell, however, is himself in his days of wavering about whether or not to be baptized.

He concludes his article with a strong defense of the need at present for people to become Christians. "Ignorance is forgivable, but the pretense of ignorance is not." He expresses pity also for those who fail to see that heaven begins on earth in the experience of Jesus Christ.[15]

A series of striking *abhangs* on Tukaram brings out the difficulty of this issue most clearly. Mixed with praise of Tukaram and his *bhakti* is a mocking of his emotionalism and lack of clear knowledge of God. Tukaram is a saint, and at the mention of his name love floods Tilak's heart. Yet only Jesus spoke with a clear voice about God, and only He is the Savior.[16] Tilak spoke similarly of past Hindu spiritual leaders in the *Christayana*: "They are far from Thee, and yet they are Thy devotees—none need doubt this; they are genuine saints who live for Thee."[17]

Tilak has rightly rejected the despicable practice of some Christians in consigning all and sundry to hell without a trace of compassion. His restraint in this area is faithful to the early disciples of Christ who did not glory in the damnation of Judas but affirmed only that he had gone to "his own place" (Acts 1:25).[18] Tilak should perhaps have shown similar restraint in nominating people for heaven, especially in the light of his Lord's clear words to the Samaritan woman that "salvation is from the Jews" (John 4:22).[19] Tilak's certainty that Hindus were saved goes beyond any teaching of Jesus or the Bible. An explanation of biblical principles such as he gave, coupled with refusal to make unwarranted decisions, seems the best approach to this emotionally and theologically difficult issue.

Social and Political Activities

Esteem for the ancient Indian heritage could not exist without vibrant concern for modern India. Tilak was clearly in two minds about social and political activity. He could not stay away from the burning issues of the time, yet was convinced that spiritual answers were far more important.

He expresses regret over some of his activities in this letter from 1915:

> I still believe so [that Christian activity should permeate all spheres of life], but I have found by experience that this belief is beset with dangers. I with this belief went ahead and identified myself with so many different activities that ultimately I found myself too much engrossed with them to be free and inclined to commune with God, to think of my own spiritual well-being, and to do direct and actual Christian duties like preaching the gospel and helping a weak or erring brother. I experienced a kind of spiritual hunger with no earnest desire to satisfy it. It was a terrible state of mind, but thank God that He touched my heart and I retraced from the folly. I kept no proportion while meddling with various human activities, and that was the folly. This led me to think and act without Christ, while my motto was "With Christ everywhere," and all this had its effect on my disposition.[20]

A later letter to his son speaks still more strongly:

> I believe that, unless India follows Jesus Christ, all her efforts to improve her status will ultimately fail. I am exclusively and wholly a preacher of Jesus and Him crucified. I repent to have wasted much of my life in trying to serve my country by taking part in all her different activities. Jesus was a patriot and wished to serve His country, and He tried to lay for its future structure the foundation of the Kingdom of God. Without that foundation civilisation itself may prove a way to utter destruction.[21]

How wholeheartedly Tilak concluded this must be questioned, however. Lakshmibai states that in his last years he was involved with the "Deccan Rayat Samaj among the non-Christians of the lower castes," seeking their uplift.[22]

The last article he submitted to *Dnyanodaya* indicated his willingness to get involved again in socio-political action. He desired someone else to do it due to his poor health and lack of organizational skills, but committed himself, if God raised him up again, to "this sacred cause" of a "Servants of the Empire" society.[23]

It is quite shocking to read Tilak's praise of and utter loyalty to the British empire from a post-Independence perspective. This is surely the area where he was most influenced by the Christian prejudices of his time. Tilak was a militant patriot, yet his vision was for an India always within the British framework. He wrote numerous articles and poems praising the Raj and praying for God's blessing on the empire.

Tilak joined the Home Rule Movement in 1916, but later resigned due to extremist tendencies in it. His pleas for caution included a disagreement with Mahatma Gandhi, whom he esteemed as "truly worthy of the title *Mahatma*."[24] India, however, in Tilak's opinion was "not yet spiritually fit" for the non-violent program Gandhi represented, and Gandhi must see and acknowledge his mistake.

Tilak might be right at this point as Gandhi's campaign was just beginning, and Gandhi did later stop it due to violence breaking out. But Tilak is sadly wrong in his wild optimism for British rule. He maintained and desired in others "a firm faith in British institutions like Parliament, and in both British and Indian officials." He spoke of the "benign British rule" and the "democratising influence of British law which works always for the common good."[25] It should be noted that the horrible massacre at Jallianwala Bagh in the Punjab that turned much moderate Indian opinion against the British had occurred only the month before these statements, which were some of Tilak's last words. Had he known of the full horror and repercussions of that event it may have begun to change some of his opinions.

Tilak's love for India could not be doubted in spite of his pro-British sentiments. He undoubtedly contributed in a wholesome way to the political and social issues he addressed, but perhaps should have acted on his sense of regret and given himself fully to Christian ministry. His political opinions are now dated and seem inept. His last step of faith in his ministry and discipleship to Christ remains valid and demands a response from the present generation.

Ah! with a tide I cannot stem
Break forth my tears, when I behold
My country e'en as Christ, 'tis told,
Gazed weeping on Jerusalem.

And from these tears of my sad spring
Blossoms the tree of Love, and showers
In lavish sweetness heavenly flowers
About Thy feet, my Loving King.

Yea, gleaming at Thy feet doth shine
My garland fitly offered,
Of all the tears which I have shed,
Mourning o'er this dear land of mine.

And all the tears which yet shall be
I offer them into Thy hand,
And with them give my Motherland
And mine own worthless self to Thee.

Now, Father, may this fancy vain
Never henceforth my mind invade,
That service to my country paid
And service done to Thee are twain.

All life is one. 'Tis only we
Sever 'twixt sacred and profane,
"Moral" and "spiritual" plane,
'Twixt nation and community.

Christ is the life of all that is;
Dharma and artha both is He, —
Both nation and community
Spirit and moral righteousness.[26]

Chapter 11

Sannyasa

Tilak's commitment to personal Christ-likeness and to Indian expressions of the Christian faith continually deepened throughout his life. Both reached a dramatic climax in his final months of life. Lakshmibai wrote,

> Tilak's nature now began to undergo increasing change with great rapidity. From earliest childhood there had been a constant ferment in his mind. He felt there was no use in remaining as one was. To the last moment he desired to be something better, and at last gained the victory over the very great faults within himself. ... Ten or twelve years before [his death] he had said, "Oh Lord, I am still extremely lacking. I have not freed myself in the least from the debts of my brothers and sisters. Oh Saviour of the unholy, I shall ever remain indebted to Thee," and he made prodigious efforts to fill up what was wanting. Many of the faults with which he had been born, thus slowly disappeared, and in this last year it would be no exaggeration to say they vanished completely.[1]

It was especially pride and anger that had haunted Tilak throughout his life, but in these last years the anger was purified to a righteous indignation and the pride dissolved away at the feet of Jesus.[2] This breaking free from besetting sins cannot be isolated, however, from the larger events of Tilak's life which helped motivate the recommitment to a more Christ-like life.

Failure in Ministry Among Hindus

Incidents where Tilak successfully led others to join him in devotion to Christ have been noted, but numerous failures clearly stirred his mind to consider what it truly meant to follow Christ. Reflecting on ministry to educated Indians, Tilak told this story:

> It was less than a month ago, that the writer met an educated non-Christian Indian leader. He was frank enough to say that he was the greatest opponent of Christ and Christianity in India. He was burning with love for his country; and wanted to know how he could best serve her cause. He found out that the writer was as good a lover of his country as he himself was, and soon was quite at home with him. He was impressed in a few days with the fact that for the real and permanent elevating of all races in India, the true conception of man must be realized, the relation of man and man must be reconstructed on the basis of the fatherhood of God, the individual must be free to form his own relation to God and man, and a way must be paved for society to proceed on liberal and moral lines. All this he soon was ready to learn of Christ, but he was not willing to confess Him or acknowledge His help. He was not afraid of caste, had little faith in idols, but he was one of the many Orientals who turn from Christ because of the un-Christian history of Western nations.
>
> There are many such men scattered through the length and breadth of India. They are all held back by a kind of political pride and prejudice, which disappears to some extent if they fall in with a Christian preacher who really loves them and thus knows how to help them.[3]

A few years later in sharing of successful ministry, he notes again the too common disappointment:

> Rev. N. V. Tilak, in reporting his literary and educational work, says: "It has been my privilege to preach the Gospel by writing letters. Each letter goes forth with prayer. This method of preaching has led four Brahmins to embrace Christianity. One of these was a Sanyasi, or "Holy Man," a speaker of three different dialects, who has wandered through the length and breadth of India in search of the truth. There are a dozen more enquirers in correspondence. A sad experience in connection with some of these men is that they stop correspondence as soon as they are convinced of the truth of Christianity, and a few go so far as to try and forget all acquaintance with me in order to avoid the final step. But my prayers for these never cease, and I feel prayer is more effective than preaching, oftentimes."[4]

New Vision

Tilak's keen intellect could not have missed that what held many back from following Christ was not rejection of the biblical Christ but rather objection to various of the western paraphernalia that are associated with discipleship to Jesus. A yet later incident of a similar nature led to the last radical step in Tilak's pilgrimage in Christ. In a March 1916 letter to his son Tilak explained the incident that eventually led to his total break from established patterns of Christian service.

> Last month, as I sat in the train at [Ahmed]Nagar station, an old man came and saluted me. He was a Brahmin who knew me intimately some thirty years ago. After some formal talk, he told me how he and many others like him felt when they heard the news of my baptism. They all thought that I was a traitor, not only to Hinduism but also to India, my own dear land. He said that his misunderstanding and intense hatred were the measure

of the real and intense love and respect they feel on seeing that I am still a genuine lover of my country. ... But
all, he said, were sorry that I should be a Christian. He
himself was sorry, because he felt that as a Hindu I had
in me both the spirit and magnetism of any great sadhu
of India, which as a Christian I had lost. He reminded
me of the fact that scores of people, both great and small,
were attracted by me, and followed me like lamps when
yet I was so young and imperfect, and asked me what
became of all that great magnetic power in me. I did not
know what to say. I simply kept quiet. I could not preach
anything to him, because his remarks had made me fully
conscious of what I was and what I am, and had humbled
me to the dust, as I looked at my present state and at
Jesus, the Life and Light of the world. He soon left me,
as if giving me a new message and creating a turning-
point in my life. I was at once upon my knees, buried
deep in prayer, meditation and communion with God,
and thinking of the whole history of my life. I awoke as
from a trance, a new man, believing that God wills to
make me a living likeness of Jesus for India, and from
that moment till now I enjoy a change and joy which
words cannot adequately express.[5]

The two greatest crises of Tilak's life were precipitated
by unexpected meetings on train journeys. While he was a
leader of the new Hinduism, a meeting with a missionary
had led to his conversion to Christianity. Now that he is a
deeply respected Christian leader, a meeting with a Hindu
leads to a radical reconversion to a Hindu way of life while
maintaining full loyalty to Jesus Christ.

The general direction of the new call that Tilak now
sensed was obvious enough; he had seen and to some extent
acted on it already long ago. A letter of July 5, 1916, shares
his developing convictions:

Fad, dream, or ideal whatever it may be called by different
persons, my God is fast leading me on to *fulfil* it. I know,

nay I trust that I am the elected Christian Tukaram for Maharashtra, a Tukaram and a St. Paul blended together. I trust hundreds will follow me, and they will form their own ... church within the churches imposed on India, but useful in giving us so many patterns of Church polity or government. I know I shall be soon a friend of all missions, a free bird just able to soar high, just leaving the happy shelter of its mother's wings (I mean the American Marathi Mission), free to be led by God alone, and to work exactly on Indian lines, and Indian tradition & principles. India needs a Christian Personality, which must be willing to accept poverty, welcome persecution, to embrace death, and in dying to say "It is fulfilled" and to "live" after death. ...

I have been in my Church & especially in the mission as a bird in its egg under the wings of its mother-bird, but I have been always careful never to borrow my light from others. Those men who borrow their light from others, never lead the human race through great crises; they who depend on the strength they gather from men and institutions are never equal to lofty achievements. The minds which electrify others, generate their own fire. But such men can not, and will hardly attend to details, and small things, they are far above them, and if they are not made free from the labyrinth of little concerns, they wither away like a beautiful flower in woods.

Hesitation

It is easy to look back and see Tilak's whole life leading up to this last step into a new pattern for ministry among Hindus. But in his own situation it was very difficult to step out into areas never before (nor, tragically, since) explored in Indian missions. Tilak did not hurry as this letter from July 24 indicates:

I am at present studying, and meditating on, the life of St. Paul, not for others but for my own personal guidance

and help. I am doing it humbly and prayerfully. ... God
has been leading me, where I can't say just now, but I
can say towards some larger service. India needs Christ,
not so much Christianity, and Christ she is to get in and
through Indian apostles, as God raises them. I am praying
for this.[6]

Tilak had now fully concluded that work within the
existing churches could never reach his beloved countrymen
for Christ. A radical break was needed, a new pattern of
life and ministry, a new brotherhood that would be truly
Indian yet still loyal to Christ. Tilak himself would be the
man to start, "a Tukaram and a St. Paul blended together."
He would leave his employment with the mission and in
step with ancient Indian tradition enter *sannyasa*, the last of
four stages in Hindu life. Tilak, like a multitude of *sannyasis*
before him, would forsake all worldly ties and devote all
his time and energy to God. But it would be another year
before he finally took the decisive steps. Tilak was not naive
about the opposition he was likely to face. Lakshmibai records
his saying

See, the time is coming when these Christian people and
missionaries will turn against me, but I shall continue to
do and say what I think is for their good. I can endure
persecution, and shall labour for their profit till I die.[7]

Tilak's son Dattu was facing decisions about post-graduate
studies or seeking work, and this no doubt added to pressure
on Tilak. These were days when *Christayana* was supposedly
top priority. The Tilaks left Ahmednagar in September of
1916 to settle in Satara, and a major reason was to create
time for the writing of the epic. But Lakshmibai remained
in poor health and Tilak wrote to his son in October that, "I
cannot proceed with the *Christayana* with real zest and zeal
with [your] Mama by my side." In early December of 1916
Tilak was invited to spend some months in America, prob-

ably in 1918. He was inclined to go and others encouraged
him to do so; in the end his new call overruled both the
writing of *Christayana* and the call to America.[8]

A letter to Dattu on February 20, 1917, shows again
Tilak's fundamental conviction and resolve and mentions
his inability to act:

> I confess I am unable to interpret your dream. But it
> shows that the consciousness of India underlying all its
> new activities is touched with the Spirit of God and that
> India is being led to Jesus, the true life of nations, without
> her knowledge. Mr. Tilak's *Gitarahasya* or *karmayoga*, Mr.
> Vaidya's new Hindu Missionary Society, Swami Ram
> Tirtha's quasi-Christian teachings, the Brahmosamajist's
> Christianity incognito, the new social movements are all
> attempts to have Christianity without Christ and stamped
> with the stamp of Hinduism. This putting new wine
> into old bottles will not do. What India now needs is the
> repetition of its religious history. She needs Christian
> Tukarams, Christian Chaitanyas, Christian Tulsidas,
> because India wise or ignorant has followed men, and she
> shall follow men and never mere doctrine, which she
> will enjoy intellectually, pervert materially, and abuse
> literally. Men she needs. She needs me, needs me to go
> about as my Lord, having nowhere to lay down his head,
> as my Lord a friend of publicans and sinners, as my Lord
> to whom to eat & drink was to do the will of his father
> in heaven, as my Lord walking meekly but bravely to
> the cross. I know it, I have been dying for it, but alas!
> what holds me back I yet fully know not! My Lord had
> three years and odd to fulfill his mission, I pray may I
> have much less than that, but I must have it before I am
> called away from this world. I am happy and blessed
> that your mother, my wife and companion of life, and
> yourself and Tara are all filled with the same ideal with
> me, you are all for our God & for your country and how
> very rare it is in the history of the world that men of
> ideals get such favourable friends in their own families!

May God be blessed and praised for this great boon which He has conferred on me. Could I make you or my wife as they are? No! I know I could not. You all are much better, much stronger than myself in many respects because God made you so. I am to you & to the world, to myself & to my God *"pushkal ajuni una"* ["still very imperfect yet," well known lines from a Tilak hymn]! All this helps me in this that it keeps me conscious of special divine help and grace to me, and of the fact that I am a poor, miserable worm that God hath chosen for His glory & service.

Tilak's appreciation for his family was vast and deep. He was indeed richly blessed by God in them, but it must also be pointed out that he had worked to win them and earn their favor. The years of Lakshmibai's ill health were not easy, yet he could write to Tara on October 5, 1916, "everyone can speak and behave in such a way as not to hurt [your] Mama's feelings. In short I advise you most earnestly and affectionately to follow me in your conduct towards Mama." The correspondence reveals Tilak as an exceptionally praiseworthy father.[9]

Pioneering Steps

Through the first half of 1917 Tilak continued to hesitate, seeing the cost and feeling the pressure of friends to stay in the old patterns. In July or early August of 1917 Tilak received a vision of Christ, something too sacred ever to share in detail. He resigned from mission service in the strength of that vision. An *abhang* gives the fullest description of the vision he ever recorded:

Ye ask and so to tell ye I am bold;
Yea, with these eyes did I the Christ behold—
Awake, not sleeping, did upon Him gaze,
And at the sight stood tranced with amaze.

"My mind wanders," I said, "it cannot be!
'Tis but my own creation that I see!
Poor hapless fool!"—for so I did repine—
"How crooked and perverse a faith is mine!"
Yet was my patient Lord displeased not,
Nor for one moment He His child forgot:
Again He came and stood regarding me;—
Ah, surely ne'er was mother such as He!
I called to Him in sudden agony.
"My child," He answered, "Wherefore dost thou cry?
I am before thee, yea, and I within;
Merged in a sea of blindness hast thou been."
"Lord, grant me eyes to see!" I cried again,
And clasped His feet in ecstasy of pain.
He raised me up, He held me to His side,
And then—I cannot tell what did betide;
But this alone I know, that from that day
This self of mine hath vanished quite away.
Great Lord of yoga, Thou hast yoked with Thee,
Saith *Dasa*, even a poor wight like me![10]

The first public notice of this decision was a brief statement Tilak read at a Christian convention and had printed
in *Dnyanodaya*:

> For the sake of my Country, for the sake of Christ's *Darbar*,
> and for my own sake, I must be free, except in love and
> service, of all human agencies, and must be bound entirely
> and to all purposes to Christ and the gospel; I therefore
> in response to God's voice, cease from this day forth to be
> a Mission agent or to be anyone's dependent or servant.
> I am a Christian *Sannyasi*, which means a follower of
> *Anuraga* [love, loyalty] and never of *Viraga* [detachment],
> and try to be and do as I am bid by God the Spirit.[11]

His full resignation letter, and the response by the mission, were printed in *Dnyanodaya*:

Satara, 6th Sept. 1917

To the Members of the American Marathi Mission

My Dear Ladies and Gentlemen,

It is with feelings of the deepest gratitude and of the most earnest love and affection that I take this opportunity to state that the American Marathi Mission has been elected and enabled by God to be a spiritual mother to me and to prepare me for higher service of God and man. Then under its auspices and with its blessing I request to be relieved to do that service.

The war, its moral consequences in the world, the new life and new angle of vision which it has diffused in nations, the new aspect of the mode of the world's thought and will, all this affecting India, has made India quite ripe and quite ready to accept the great originator and helper of human life, social, political, moral and spiritual, Jesus Christ.

But India will go after a man, a man elected by God to meet her ideals. Most humbly, but most firmly, I state to you and to the world that God has elected me, a weak sinner, for this purpose. This election requires my resigning a salary from the Mission or from any other human agency. So far I resign from the Mission, but never in other respects, if I possess a grain of gratefulness. I am and ever shall be the same friend and servant of the Mission, to do all things required of me as before.

I have already announced that I am so far free, and I hope and request that I may get a formal consent from you as soon as possible.

I beg to remain, Ladies and Gentlemen,

Your most grateful servant,

N. V. Tilak

Ahmednagar, 9th Sept. 1917

To Rev. N. V. Tilak,
From The Members of the American Marathi Mission,

Our Beloved Brother,

We have read with deep emotion your letter of Sept. sixth requesting to be relieved from paid service in our Mission, but expressing your desire and determination to remain connected with it for fellowship and service, and to work under its auspices.

As you express gratitude for what the Mission and its members have been to you, so we express gratitude to our common divine Father for what through you He has done for us personally, for our Indian Christian brothers and sisters, and for our beloved India.

We respect and appreciate your conviction that our India urgently needs Indian Christians who feel called of God and moved to promote her spiritual life through service which appears to them to be in accord with Indian ideals and Indian methods involving renunciation of all assured support from any organization and from any men.

In these days of India's spiritual travail our great, good God who has chosen you and guided you hitherto will continue to guide and strengthen you for great service. Be assured of our individual and united love and interest in you and in your family. Our hearts, our homes, our hopes, our prayers, our co-operation are ever, ever yours in service for our divine Lord in our beloved India.

In behalf of all the members of the American Marathi Mission.

Yours very affectionately,

R. A. Hume[12]

Writing in this way Tilak was careful to make clear that he held nothing against the mission. It was equally made

clear that the Hindu pattern of *sannyasa* would not be slav-
ishly followed, but altered somewhat by biblical principles.[13]
The mission in gratitude for Tilak's years of service granted
him a house for himself and his family. He put on the saffron
robe of the renunciant, keeping two which he himself washed.
Tilak often wandered the countryside meeting people as a
traditional *sannyasi*, but broke from the *sannyasa* pattern in
having a permanent home. The "home" was named Christayana Ashram, apparently the first Christian ashram, and
this became the focal point of the new work.

Rather than leaving his family as in traditional *sannyasa*,
Tilak was supported by his family who joined him in this
step of faith. He ceased normal marital relations with his
wife, however. Tilak answered some questions about this
in *Dnyanodaya*:

> Christian *sannyasa* in no way means forsaking one's wife,
> but rather that she should love you and you should love
> her selflessly, and that following Christ's will and teach-
> ing you should both take your mutual relationship into
> heaven right here on earth. ... St. Paul, who gives the
> divine message to the world, counts self control among
> the fruits of the Holy Spirit (Gal. 5:22,23). ... Christian
> renunciation does not enjoin the husband to abandon
> his wife. In this respect, the Lord's clear injunction is,
> "Let not what God has joined together be put asunder."
> In brief, if your family, which is already beyond your
> means, is to increase still further, then do not take *sannyasa*
> as I have. Rather, take God's help and, either gradually
> or at one go, give up *eros* which is linked with *agape* in
> regard to your wife. ... This is elementary renunciation.
> For it to become total, the cooperation of both husband
> and wife is needed. The more that both of you become
> engrossed in meditation, prayer, and the service of God,
> the more will such *sannyasa* become easily attainable. ...
> Do not complacently take my, or any human being's,
> advice. To do so is a sign that you are dependent upon

humans, and not yet upon God. And remember one more thing. "Let only those who can, accept this" (Matt. 19:12). ... Besides, if we properly think on the section 1 Cor. 12:4-20, it will be seen that those who are incapable of such great sacrifices are in no wise less than those who have made them. It is sufficient if, in the condition in which we are, we have used the strength and means which we have for God and people. Then, our worthiness and our usefulness are not a whit less than those who make these great sacrifices. ... What you, or some other people call my "instability," I understand to be a gift of divine grace, and I have often thanked God for it.[14]

This *sannyasa* in the steps of Christ would not emphasize *viraga* (renunciation and detachment) as in Hinduism, but rather *anuraga* (loving attachment and service). The traditional *sannyasi* survived by begging, but this was violently repudiated. Tilak explained,

Your family is large, and if you by taking *sannyasa* force your progeny to beg for their food that will be a great sin. There are many places in the holy scriptures where the commands and counsels carrying the sense of "God sees to the welfare of his devotees, hence they ought not to worry about their livelihood" may be found. But the world has not yet properly understood the meaning of even a single one of those statements. To put it in a nutshell, the sum and substance of them all is in this single saying of Christ, "The laborer is worthy of his hire." ... Who is the master of these laborers that will pay them their wages? Obviously, the Lord. But through whom will he arrange to give these wages? That world which these laborers will serve. How much? In proportion to the importance of their labor. From this you will grasp that ... for a Christian *sannyasi* who serves the world, to hold out his mendicant's sack is not to behave as a beggar. "To hold out the beggar's bowl! Away with such shameful living!" The Christian *sannyasi* will never ever do that.

I have had recourse to the mendicant's sack because I am prepared to serve India. I want the wages of my service, but I require it in the due measure of that service. Even if someone were to place before me a hundred thousand rupees because they saw my family and felt pity for them, I would not want the money. If the world were to assess the value of my service only in keeping with my own stomach, I would remain hungry and set that food before my family. If the assessment were sufficient to feed ten families, I too would sit at table with my family and eat a few mouthfuls. What remained I would return to the world, for it belongs to the world. We find terrible the plague which has beset our country for 21 years now, but there is an epidemic more terrible than that which has been endlessly besetting our country. Beggary is the name of this epidemic! ... If it is possible for you to support yourself and your family, and only to the extent that your profession ... does not come in the way of your service of God and country, then most certainly relinquish your salary, and become free.[15]

Tilak was certain that only in this type of Christian *sannyasa* could the true gospel of the true Christ be preached and win true disciples from among the Hindus. He highlighted seven biblical truths that must be present in the life of a Christian *sannyasi*. No one who had been excommunicated by a church or criminally convicted by a civil court could join the new brotherhood.[16]

God's Darbar

So at 55 years of age Tilak embarked on the greatest adventure of his life. He began "God's *darbar*" (*Devacha darbar*, "the royal court of God"), which he described as "a brotherhood of the baptized and unbaptized disciples of Christ."[17] For Tilak was convinced, as J. C. Winslow wrote, that

> If Christ could be presented to India in His naked beauty, free from the disguises of Western organisation, Western doctrines and Western forms of worship, India would acknowledge Him as the supreme Guru, and lay her richest homage at His feet. He believed that there were already thousands of his fellow-countrymen who, while unwilling to accept the stigma of denationalization which the acceptance of Christian baptism seemed to imply, were yet at heart true disciples of the Christ, and that some society was needed which should band together all such true disciples, whether baptized or unbaptized, in a single brotherhood.[18]

Tilak saw that his goal of contextualizing the Christian message did not in any way mean a compromise of the gospel of Christ, but on the contrary would highlight the true spirit of the gospel which was so often hidden from the eyes of the Indian people. The work of a *darbari* (member of the brotherhood) included serving the church, and the goals of the *darbar* explicitly included the renewal of the church so that it would become truly Indian.

All *darbaris* agreed to nine commitments:

1. I have made Christ my guru. Hence, I shall meditate on his life, character, purposes, and preaching.

2. In order to be able to properly do such meditation, I shall study the Bible and other books on this subject (1 Pet. 2:2).

3. The Lord Jesus Christ is saying to his disciples, "I am your life." I shall accordingly take him along with me in all I think and do (Jn. 15:4).

4. At the start, in the middle, and at the end of my daily schedule, that is, in the morning, at noon, and before going to bed at night, I shall pray to the one and only holy God, whose nature is love, and who is my Father (Mt. 7:7–8).

5. I shall consider every member of the *darbar* as my brother or sister. … In brief, henceforward my motto will be this alone: That the world, when it sees the fraternal love of the *darbaris* of the Devacha (God's) Darbar, may be filled with wonder and give glory to God (Mt. 12:47–50; Jn. 17:21).

6. I shall attend divine worship once a week, and worship with any other *darbaris* who may be in the neighborhood, on a day and at a time that has been decided with them.

7. I shall regularly perform some kind of selfless service (*nishkam seva*) for people.

8. On the understanding that all responsibilities of the *darbar* are my own, I shall contribute money regularly as well as on special occasions.

9. Every twelve months I shall bring into the *darbar* at least one new member.[19]

There was an associate membership for those not ready for this full commitment, and a group of friends of the *darbar*. For the evangelists and preachers of the *darbar* this vow to Christ was to be affirmed:

Like Thee, O Christ, I will remain poor.

Like Thee I will serve.

Like Thee I will be the friend of all, the enemy of none.

Like Thee I will ever be ready to be nailed to a cross.

Like Thee I will strive fully to do the will of God.

Like Thee I will love all mankind.

In the strength of faith I will abide in Thy presence. Thy world and mine shall be one. I will strive after Thy likeness, and finally, being united to Thee, by my own personal experience I will prove to be true that saying of Paul, the chief of saints, "Ye died, and your life is hid with Christ in God."[20]

This plan contains much of significance and greatness, and had it been fully implemented the results may have been far reaching. It cannot be a surprise that such an effort drew criticism from many Christians. Tilak's ire at such rumor-mongering and uncharitable judgments by Christians is vividly portrayed by Lakshmibai.[21]

Tilak died within 20 months of beginning the *darbar*, having about 50 Christian people with him at that point.[22] His plan centered so much on himself that with his death the *darbar* also died. Despite the *darbar's* short life span, Tilak's program for it and his resolve in implementing it certainly demand that Tilak be recognized as one of the outstanding pioneers of mission history.

Henceforth

Henceforth you are mine, O Lord,
Beloved brother, master (swami) and king; henceforth.   (refrain)

Your service is my food; meditation on you is my sleep; henceforth.
Shouting out your name is the breath of my life; henceforth.
My eyes grow dim towards worldly things and are fixed on your feet;
Lord, you are mine; Lord, you are mine;
Beloved brother, master and king; henceforth.

For you I give up my home and all ties of relationship; for you I give up
all worldly affairs; henceforth.
For you I give up all my bodily life; I place everything under your control;
henceforth.
I offer to you myself and all that I am. I give all to you; Lord, take it.
Lord, you are mine; Lord, you are mine;
Beloved brother, master and king; henceforth.

You are my thought (vichar), my speech (ukti), my knowledge (yukti),
enjoyment (bhukti), salvation (mukti); henceforth.
Now no longer does any difference exist between us; even if there is any,
it is only superficial; henceforth.
I am free, happy, at peace, always, in heaven.
Lord, you are mine; Lord, you are mine;
Beloved brother, master and king; henceforth.[23]

Chapter 12

Final Days

Lakshmibai states that "the last year of Tilak's life ... was worth ten others."[1] He gave himself to the growth and expansion of the *darbar* and was enriched and encouraged at positive responses to his vision:

> God ordains that the Darbar should take up aggressive work. I am no more in difficulties of men. Two Indian Christian graduates & an under-graduate of whom two are ladies have offered their services if they get enough to keep body & soul together. Not less than five other young persons gone as far as the vernacular school final are also ready to resign their work in missions where they get pay to their satisfaction & to come over to me if they but get enough to live. Such self-sacrifice must be at once encouraged. ... I have applied ... for a gift or a loan without interest to build here in Satara the Headquarters of the Darbar.[2]

But opposition from missionaries scuttled this plan; it seems Tilak took a unilateral decision to leave Satara without raising any controversy with his antagonists.[3]

Reflections on Death

The *darbar* would never have a headquarters, as Tilak's final illness had begun. Knowing and believing the Bible as he did, Tilak could not look on death with sadness, nor as a final end. His death came quite unexpectedly, but there was enough forewarning that he was able to record clearly his own perspective and wishes.

Tilak disapproved of the standard Christian practice of draping everything in black on the death of a loved one, and forbade such to be done when he died. He said to Lakshmibai,

> Should it be an unhappy thing to go to God? Can it be a misfortune to go to Him who is immortal and holy? Which is suggestive of holiness, black or white? If I go before you, you are not to do any of these things. Let everything connected with me be white. ... When I am gone, you or the children must not mourn for me at all. I am convinced that I must go to God, and that there is no cause for sorrow in my going. He will take me and He will continue to look after you.[4]

His will expressed themes that had dominated his life and to which he indeed remained true in death:

> If it is the wish of my friends and relatives to put up a tombstone over the spot where my body is laid, on that stone should be carved the line "Still very imperfect, Lord; very imperfect am I yet." Before my name no title whatsoever should be written. ... They should not write N. V. Tilak in the English way, but Narayan Vaman Tilak in Marathi; in all earnestness I say to my friends and relations, that they must take the utmost care to see that the word poet, or any other title of respect, is not inserted.
>
> No one knows when his calling will come from God, and no one should waste time in futile thought about it. I shall never describe the call of God as "Death," because

it is to be called of God, God's calling. It is an awakening to new life. When thoughts of death come into my mind I never feel despondent. "No trouble while dying, no trouble while living." This is the right of the Christian man, and in Christ I have had experience of it beyond all conceiving. I think I have not loved Father, Mother, wife or children, friend or even myself as much as I love my country. The Indian Christian must be made to ponder deeply upon the growth of the Church, the making of it truly free, and the filling of it with life.[5]

On December 4, 1918, he wrote other of his views and wishes to the daughter of his old mentor, Dr. R. A. Hume:

I am suddenly become so very sick with a pain in my heart that I think I shall be called away any moment tonight. I am quite ready. I leave the following wishes and messages:

1. The Mission, I hope, will take care of my wife. She is an angel, but she has her weaknesses, will you be her sister?

2. *Christayana* is incomplete. Help Tara, and try to develop her poetical inspiration, that she may finish it one day.

3. Do not make much of me anywhere when I am gone. I have not accomplished one thousandth part of what God made me capable of accomplishing. I wish nothing from you all or from the world but pardon. ...

My messages:

1. To India: Follow Jesus.

2. To my Christian Brothers and Sisters: Your life is in Christ; your life is in Him and nothing else.

3. To Missionaries: Cease to be fathers and mothers, be real brothers and sisters. Know how to appreciate, trust people and take the place of India's revered saints.

4. To all: I lived as a friend and died as a friend of all, and I am still, both here and hereafter.[6]

Illness and Death

Tilak had long had chronic hemorrhoids, first mentioned in a letter of August 6, 1914. The last months of his life he was constantly in and out of pain, and in and out of hospitals. Lakshmibai wrote that "sometimes Tilak would give addresses, but sometimes he used to be so overcome with pain that I was terrified."[7] When surgery seemed appropriate it had to be delayed because Tilak contracted bronchitis. He wrote on April 16, 1919, that

> Neither doctor nor I can tell you whether I am improving. But one thing is certain, and that is, "Blessed, doubly blessed, is all this pain; it is experiencing the cross in my body. Blessed, thrice blessed, is this sickness; it is perfect union with Christ." With Christ, and in Him, all my pain disappears; it comes again when I miss Him. The doctor and all here wonder at it. I am, with all my sickness, as it were, the pastor of the hospital! Praise God with me.[8]

On April 24 he wrote on a post card to his son that "the month of April 1919 is a wonderful month in all my life to me, it is full of *vish* [poison] and *amrit* [nectar of eternal life]. The latter predominates."

On May 9, 1919, Narayan Vaman Tilak died in J. J. Hospital in Bombay. His family was with him, Lakshmibai and Devdatt at his side when he passed from this life to glory. No clear cause of death could be determined. His wishes were fulfilled in the funeral arrangements, with a large assembly of both Christians and Hindus gathering in a Bombay church for his memorial service. During his final illness Tilak wrote this *abhang* on facing death:

O Brother, on my shoulder rests Thy hand,
　　And fearless waits my soul;
O Way, erect on Thee I take my stand,
　　And radiant gleams my goal;

O Truth, within the warmth of Thine embrace,
   All doubts dissolving die;
O Life, before the sunshine of Thy face,
   Death perisheth, not I!
Thy servant saith, Today there draweth near
   That latest valley,—and wherefore should I fear?[9]

Following the memorial service the coffin was carried to Worli crematorium. The crowd in procession along the way was led by Lakshmibai, singing Tilak's own hymn:[10]

What fear hath he whose Master is the Lord,
Whose heart and mind can form no alien thought,
Who speaketh of the Lord his God alone,
Who liveth in this world to bless the world,
But owneth no allegiance to the world?
His poverty is here his sole reward,
But the wealth of Heaven is his to hold.
His body is his own, but therein dwells
Not his own soul, but lo, the Soul of Christ.
Beneath his conquering foot lie agonies
Of heart and flesh, and even Death dies there.[11]

The ashes were collected and were buried after a special service during a Christian convention on October 24, 1919, in the Indian Christian cemetery in Ahmednagar.

The Soul's Passing

When my last sleep shall come,
Take Thou my head into Thy lap and fold Thine arms about me.
So let me rest, gazing up into Thy Face, my Mother-Father.
Thus at the last, of Thy mercy, let me breathe out my life.
The Servant says — I ask but this.
Fulfill, O Beloved, this my last desire.[12]

Chapter 13

Epilogue

N. V. Tilak's conversion and early ministry illustrate many points of inadequacy and failure in Christian communication to and interaction with Hindus. Tilak is one of the most illustrious among a truly noble band of men and women who have sought to follow Christ without rejecting their Hindu religio-cultural heritage. In his closing years Tilak demonstrated a pattern of witness for Christ among Hindus that must be counted as one of the great experiments in church and mission history.

Extraction vs. Incarnation

It was inevitable that on becoming a Christian Tilak would be ripped out of his society, to the anguish of all involved. This will continue to happen as long as Christian evangelists stand outside the Hindu culture and call Hindus to come out to them and the church.

This extraction of a disciple of Christ from his society is entirely unnecessary, however. The biblical pattern of ministry is to enter another's culture and live there. Had any missionary adopted the Hindu lifestyle of Tilak, he could have remained in his culture rather than spend 21 years in exile from it. Sadly, Tilak's early death prevented him from demonstrating the viability of his new approach.

Tilak's death ended God's *darbar*, an effort rich in potential but which in practice failed. But, as J. C. Winslow pointed out, "if it failed, it was a splendid failure; and it will not have failed if it supplies an inspiration and points a way which others may follow."[1] It is tragic that more than 75 years after Tilak's death no similar movement has begun. Is it too much to hope that Tilak might yet speak so long after his death and inspire a new generation to follow his example?

Reflections on God's Darbar

It is easy to criticize aspects of God's *darbar*. It's utter dependence on Tilak himself left it without hope on his demise. Tilak perhaps stressed too much his own role as apostle, and new pioneers in his footsteps must beware of thinking too highly of themselves. But could the *darbar* have been much different? Under any structure it could not have gone on without Tilak.

The *darbar* sought a middle road, wanting both to transform the church and reach into Hindu society. The close ties with the church surely alienated Hindus, and how soon this situation might have improved can only be guessed. It is highly doubtful that a transdenominational fellowship would have survived for any significant length of time. Rich blessing and numerical increase would surely have led to a new church movement or to some sort of Christocentric Hindu *sampradaya* (religious order, sect, or denomination). Since Tilak's primary concern was for communicating the message of Christ to Hindus, it would have been wise to begin at a greater distance from the existing church.[2]

On Baptism

The willingness to downplay baptism and permit the neglect of this clear command of Christ must also be noted. Baptism is certainly badly misunderstood as signifying the rejection of all that is Hindu for the acceptance of all that is "Christian," the latter including many shameful and silly actions and traditions. Something must be done about the needless offense caused by this misunderstanding. It is doubtful that eliminating the requirement of baptism would solve the problem, however. Hindu disciples of Christ would surely not be willing to live in known disobedience to their Lord's will. Even to suggest this is to despise the *bhakti* tradition of total submission and obedience to the Lord.

A better approach to the difficult baptism issue lies in dropping the transliterated Greek word *baptism* altogether. Jesus as Guru commands a *sanskara* (sacrament) with water for his disciples. He places his *diksha* or initiatory sign on all who follow him. This definition and description, coupled with *bhaktas* (devotees) living out the way of Christ in Hindu communities and contexts, would eventually break down the tragic misconceptions about Jesus' initiatory rite.[3] Quite possibly an interpretation and practice on these lines would have forced themselves on Tilak had his work gone on and prospered.

Tilak's Legacy

It must be concluded that Tilak stopped short of entering the Hindu context as fully as he might have. He could have moved further from the existing church, and embraced the name Hindu instead of Hindi. Yet he went far beyond what most have even considered, and his legacy to present disciples of Christ lies primarily in his example of radical action in entering the Hindu context. Today there is no shortage of talk about adaptation with deep sensitivity and understanding to Hindu thought and practices, but role models of Christ-*bhakti* are tragically few.

Insofar as the Indian church in the twentieth century has made an effort to adapt to its Hindu cultural context (and this has surely not been far enough), the goal has been to become both *fully Indian* and *fully Christian*. Tilak in his last years, along with a handful of other pioneers, points to a stronger, more radical goal: to be *truly Hindu* and *fully biblical*.

When by God's grace and power Hindu peoples bow in full submission to Christ, it will be effected through disciples with hearts like Tilak's, acting on principles such as he spelled out, independent of any oversight or finances from abroad. May fervent prayer for God's hastening of such a day be the response of all who read this book.

No Longer I, but Christ

Come, Jesu! Dearest Saviour, come!
  Come to this heart of mine;
And banish all which hinders me
  From being wholly Thine;
Thy mind, Thy thoughts be mine, dear Lord.
  Thine all the words I say;
Yea, suppliant at Thy feet I plead,
  Take all my self away.

. . . .

In me may all men Thee behold,
  And praise Thy grace divine;
So through me may Thy kingdom come
  No other end be mine!
O Christ, the Sun beyond compare,
  From chance and changing free,
Thy light can never fade nor set!
  All peace abides in Thee![4]

Appendix

PRAY!

by Narayan Vaman Tilak

Dnyanodaya 63, 28 Jan. 1904, 4

Sons and daughters of India, who love Christ and love their own country, pray that God may raise up apostles in India for the advancement of His kingdom, the foundation of which has been laid by his servants from the West.

Pray that volunteers from among us may come forth, who will repeat the history of India during the sixteenth and the seventeenth centuries, giving the land once more a long line of Christian Sadhus, of Christian Chaitanyas, of Christian Nanaks, of Christian Tukarams.

Pray to prove to awakening India that the Indian Christian Church is the greatest gift of God to her. Pray that the Indian Christian Church may realize the true value of her existence, and that she may grow so as to make that existence powerfully felt.

Pray to be able to bring home the truth to all Indian Christian ministers that India—half civilised as she is called—has been the follower of the ideal, and of nothing short of that, and that she is today ready to follow Christ the man of sorrows, the Son of God crucified, who is presented to the world through His disciples, as His presence in them prepares them to be themselves men of sorrows, children of God willing to be crucified for the spiritual welfare of their fellow-beings.

Pray to be made able to prove that the Christian ministry does not mean simply preaching the Gospel, but it means living Christ in public and in private, so as to sanctify every phase of life in us and around us.

Pray that the Indian Christians be prepared themselves to be soldiers of the kingdom of God.

Pray that the spirit of servitude in the Indian Christian heart be removed.

Pray that the present Indian Christian ministry be prevented from being developed into a human profession rather than a divine vocation, by creating a staff of volunteers and by creating a spiritual zeal in the Church for independent Christian service.

Pray that we may soon begin to fulfil the hopes of the Western Churches about us by trying to teach our own people to do themselves what the missionaries are doing for India, and so repay to some extent the loan of love we owe those noble Churches.

Pray to make one wonderful family of all India, one body of Christ, wherein are sanctified and amalgamated the thought of the Brahman, the simple obedience of the Shudra, the patience of the Ati-shudras (outcastes), the valour and simple honesty of the Aborigines, the adaptability and skill of the mercantile classes, the religious enthusiasm of the

Mahomedans, and the speculation of the Theosophists, the Samajists, and such other sects of new India.

Pray that volunteers from among us may rise up who love most earnestly both the Gospel and also their own country, who can exclaim with Jeremiah, "Cursed be the man that trusteth in man, and maketh flesh his arm, and whose heart departeth from the Lord"; who have love to others and prefer to say with St. Paul, "I have coveted no man's silver, or gold, or apparel. Yea, ye yourselves know, that these hands have ministered unto my necessities, and to them that were with me," and yet who, on the other hand believe that "the labourer is worthy of his hire," who are willing to co-operate, so far as possible, with all the established Missions and Churches of India, bearing always in mind that a paid agent of a Mission is as good a servant of the Lord as a volunteer. Nay, pray that the Lord may raise up such volunteers as would say with Paul, "Some indeed preach Christ even of envy and strife; and some also of good will. What then! notwithstanding every way, whether in pretence, or in truth, Christ is preached, and I therein do rejoice and will rejoice."

Pray that God may raise up apostles in India, who see and experience in their hearts all the wonderful advantages placed by our Heavenly Father at the disposal of the Indian Christian Church, and who are desirous of making the best use of them for the regeneration of their country through Jesus, the Christ.

Pray that the Lord may raise up in India, not a society, nor a machine, nor any thing resembling these, but a simple brotherhood drawn together and blended in one through the one attractive force—love for human beings.

Pray that the brave Punjab, eloquent Bengal, the meditative North, the religious Central India, the generous Gujerat, the agitating Deccan, and organizing Madras may contribute to this brotherhood both men and means, and more than all else, sympathy and prayer.

Pray that the flower of the Western Church, even the foreign missionaries, may heartily sympathize with and help this brotherhood, and be prepared to co-operate with it, and allow it, and encourage it to co-operate with them. Pray that the generous and loving Western Churches make an advance and use their power and means in bringing about an independent brotherhood in India for the annexation of the land to the Kingdom of God, a brotherhood which will be a monument of their work in India. India is poor, and the despised out-caste Indian Christian Community is still poorer; left to work out its own way through a dense labyrinth of difficulties, without the least sympathy of the people about them, who unfortunately still very bitterly hate the very name of the one and only Saviour of mankind, Jesus, who ultimately is to be the redeemer of India in all respects.

Pray, ye sons and daughters of India; pray prayerfully, incessantly, earnestly, with faith in God and with readiness to accept what He offers, not waiting to test His offers by your own human and therefore erring will.

Ahmednagar 9-1-04   N. V. Tilak

Notes

Preface pp. xi–xii

1. Ashok Devdatt Tilak, "Narayan Waman Tilak," unpublished paper, 1978, p. 17.

2. "I cannot, and none can stop or guide the pens and lips of the world, I am sorry it is so. But I wish either to be forgotten altogether by all, or to be painted just as I am" (letter of 14 Aug. 1915).

Acknowledgments pp. xiii–xiv

1. Lakshmibai's account of her life with Tilak, *Sampurna Smruti-chitre* (hereafter *Smrutichitre*) is rightfully a classic work of Marathi prose. The English translation by E. Josephine Inkster (*I Follow After* [Madras: Oxford University Press, 1950]) ends with Tilak's death, or at the end of part three of Lakshmibai's four part autobiography. It should be noted that the two most important chapters in the entire book for missiological study (chapters 15 and 17 in part three) are edited out of this English version (excepting the first few paragraphs of chapter 17 which appear on pages 316–17 at the end of English chapter 15).

2. See "A Tribute to Rev. N. V. Tilak after His Baptismal Centenary" in two parts in *Vidyajyoti Journal of Theological Reflection* 60, no. 6,7 (June, July 1996): 399–417, 443–54; and "Mehta's Movie 'Smrutichitre': Postcolonial Feminist Construct? 'Hindutvavadi' Distortion?" *Religion and Society* 43, no. 3 (Sept. 1996): 70–113.

Chapter 1: Introduction pp. 1–9

1. Christianity and Hinduism are juxtaposed here as in popular understanding of the two "religions." Heinrich von Stietencron's insight on their fundamental differences needs to be noted, however. He is first referring to differences within Hinduism itself:

Different ritual, different theology, different holy scriptures and different highest gods; it is obvious that "Hinduism" embraces differences at least as explicitly fundamental as those between Judaism, Christianity and Islam, along with other minor religions and popular cults of the Near East. If we were to subsume all these under one umbrella term as various "sects" of one Near-Eastern religion, this would give us a proper equivalent to Hinduism. But a cry of outrage from all of these religions would stop us; they would never agree to be reduced to mere sects. They never learnt to develop that measure of tolerance which is practised and—more important—theologically or anthropologically justified in Hindu religions. Therefore our choice is limited. If we accept Judaism, Christianity and Islam as "religions" and if, compelled by intellectual honesty, we want to apply the same term to comparable phenomena, we cannot avoid concluding that there are a number of different "religions" existing side by side within "Hinduism." ("Hinduism: On the Proper Use of a Deceptive Term," in *Hinduism Reconsidered*, ed. Gunther Sontheimer and Hermann Kulke [New Delhi: Manohar Publications, 1991], 16–17.)

2. *Dnyanodaya* 71, 12 Sept. 1912, 37. *See Glossary*: Dnyanodaya.

3. E. G. K. Hewat, *Christ and Western India* (Bombay: Wilson College, 1953), 49.

4. Ibid., 77, from a letter of Wilson's from 1831.

5. Quoted in E. J. Sharpe, *Faith Meets Faith: Some Christian Attitudes to Hinduism in the Nineteenth and Twentieth Centuries* (London: SCM Press, 1977), 5.

6. 50 volumes appearing from Oxford University Press 1878–1910, available still in reprinted editions.

7. The first volume, on Bhanudas, appeared in 1926. J. F. Edwards was the concluding editor of the series after the death of Justin Abbott in 1932. Published privately in Pune, some volumes have been reprinted more recently in Delhi.

8. The New Age movement that has invaded the West must be considered an offshoot of philosophical Hinduism that has little relation to actual Hinduism.

9. From *Stotramala: A Garland of Hindu Prayers*, The Poet-Saints of Maharashtra, No. 6, trans. Justin E. Abbott (Pune, India: Scottish Mission Industries, 1929), 36–37.

10. J. N. Farquhar, *The Crown of Hinduism* (Oxford: Oxford University Press, 1915).

11. From: World Missionary Conference, *The Missionary Message in Relation to Non-Christian Religions*, Report of Commission IV, Edinburgh 1910 (London: Oliphant, Anderson & Ferrier, 1910), 171 (italics in the original).

12. John 14:27, 16:33.

13. Farquhar's study also makes much of the needs of the emerging Indian nation, arguments that have lost their relevance with the passage of time.

14. Farquhar, *Crown*, 54.

15. For a helpful analysis see Eric J. Sharpe, *Not to Destroy But to Fulfil: The Contribution of J. N. Farquhar to Protestant Missionary Thought in India before 1914* (Lund, Sweden: CWK Gleerup, 1965).

16. *Dnyanodaya* 76, 24 May 1917, 21, *abhang* 50. It should be noted that this is a poetic expression; in so far as it is historically accurate it is in subliminal rather than in outwardly verifiable terms.

17. J. Z. Hodge, "The Forward Movement in Evangelism under the N.C.C.," in *Evangelism*, The Madras Series, vol. 3, Records of the International Missionary Council, 12–29 Dec. 1938 (New York), 97.

18. Sharpe, *Faith*, 132. Sharpe speaks not only of the dismissal of fulfillment ideas, but also of A. G. Hogg's anti-fulfillment thinking. Another factor beside the disintegration of Christian theology he sees as the rapid changes in the external world (political, social, etc.) in which Hinduism and Christianity met.

19. Narayan Vaman Tilak, *Bhakti Niranjana* (Nasik, India: Nagarik Press, n.d.), 29; trans. J. C. Winslow (hereafter N. V. Tilak, *Bhakti*; trans. JCW). The title means: *A Flame of Devotion*.

Chapter 2: Early Years pp. 10–13

1. Jack C. Winslow, *Narayan Vaman Tilak: The Christian Poet of Maharashtra* (Calcutta: Association Press, 1930), 14.

2. Lakshmibai Tilak, *I Follow After*, trans. E. Josephine Inkster (Madras: Oxford University Press, 1950), 15.

3. This story must be balanced by a reflection from late in life when Tilak spoke of himself in the third person:

   I know a particular man, who rarely spoke of his own departed father; and if he occasionally alluded to him, it was to illustrate how a generation ago it was thought below the dignity of a man that he should show himself attached to his own wife or to his own offspring. He had as a child reason to dislike his father nay even to feel hatred towards him, which hatred duty and any goodness in the fellow had softened into a sort of indifference which almost reached oblivion. But the man became a Christian afterwards, and began to grow in grace and the wisdom that comes from Christ. One morning he was thinking of his own son, and he wondered how the son of a hard-hearted man loved his own son so much. I have to add parenthetically that recently the man had begun to think with Christ and to try to do all things with him. Then Jesus said to him, "was your father as hard-hearted as Zacchaeus? as hard-hearted as the thief on the cross? were not these all found humane, and loving? and why? how? because I loved them; because I could catch hold of the best in them." The man at once remembered how once he was very dangerously ill and how when his father realized his state approached his pillow, caressed him and wept. Only once in all his life time the man had found his father weeping, only once near his pillow, only once caressing him, but that did not move him at all then. Now after nearly a generation, with Jesus, he knew the meaning of those tears shed only once on his account, and found out that they were far much more worth than the tears of a father if he were to shed them a thousand times. The father of the man died when he was young and now when he is almost as old as him, he loves him and cries for him and feels full of appreciation of him. (A. D. Tilak points this out in *Smrutichitre*, 791–92, but I quote the longer original from Tilak's letter of 4 Apr. 1916.)

4. Winslow, *Tilak*, 14–15.

5. N. V. Tilak, *Bhakti*, 3 (*Christayana* 1:5–6); trans. JCW.

Chapter 3: Restless Wanderer pp. 14–18

1. Incidents related about these early experiences are not easily reconciled into a coherent whole. See Winslow, *Tilak*, 10, 15–16 for example. Ashok D. Tilak traces these events to 1883–1884 and supports the suggestion that Tilak walked as far as Delhi (*Smrutichitre*, 842; cf. 77).

2. A. D. Tilak summarized his findings on Tilak's published works, but information is scant for the early period. Noteworthy here is that his first published poem appears to have been from 1882. In 1884–85 three booklets were published, the two that are known being in defense of Hinduism ("It is Not Sinful to Worship Idols," and "Government Interference Not Wanted in Hindu Peoples' Religious Practices"). The first extant work is a collection of 27 poems dating from 1885. An 1886 poetry collection features the play of Krishna with Radha and the Gopis. An 1887 account of

a Hindu saint gives uncritical mention of his miraculous works, but a similar 1889 production ignores such stories and celebrates only the oratory of a saint; 1889 also saw the play and poems on cow protection. An 1891 anthology on a goddess is striking as a number of the works were later slightly changed and used as hymns to Christ. For details see *Smrutichitre*, 804–12.

3. L. Tilak, *I Follow*, 125–26. The second and third sentences of this long quotation have been altered according to advice from Malcolm Nazareth; Inkster's translation is misleading in a minor way. It must be noted that Tilak is not entirely accurate in disclaiming all reading of the Bible, as he had read some of the Bible by this time (on this see A. D. Tilak's footnote on page 217 of *Smrutichitre*).

4. Ibid., 108.

5. Ibid., 106.

6. N. V. Tilak, *Bhakti*, 124; trans. Mrs. G. M. Chute.

Chapter 4: Conversion pp. 19–24

1. L. Tilak, *I Follow*, 126–27.

2. Ibid., 102.

3. Ibid., 109.

4. Ibid., 108.

5. Winslow, *Tilak*, 20.

6. Ibid., 21.

7. Ibid., 21.

8. L. Tilak, *I Follow*, 110.

9. Ibid., 129.

10. N. V. Tilak, *Bhakti*, 116; trans. JCW.

Chapter 5: Confusion pp. 25–31

1. *Dnyanodaya* 53, 22 Nov. 1894, 47.

2. L. Tilak, *I Follow*, 147.

3. Ibid., 134.

4. See D. Devadoss, *Life of Poet H. A. Krishna Pillai* (Madras: The Madras Law Journal Press, 1946), 38.

5. It must be noted that Tilak himself wrote about the wearing of the tuft of hair in an article in *Dnyanodaya* 69, 24 Nov. 1910, 47.

The article suggests Tilak's continued opposition to the practice as he asserts that this is a religious and not merely a national custom. He acknowledges, however, that his interpretation is from the Hindu scriptures and this meaning is forgotten in the present practice of Hindus. Thus his apparent opposition loses its validity. Undoubtedly in the last stage of his life Tilak would not have opposed this custom.

6. L. Tilak, *I Follow*, 172–73.

7. Ibid., 148.

8. From Hattie L. Bruce, "Sketch of a Brahmin Woman," an unpublished paper in the appendices of *Sampurna Smrutichitre*, 831–39; the quotation is from pp. 834–35.

9. See Lakshmibai's account of this in *I Follow*, 144–46. Details on the Hindu leaders involved are from *Smrutichitre*, 244 (cf. 735–37).

10. Bruce, "Brahmin Woman," 835.

11. L. Tilak, *I Follow*, 147.

12. These events occurred in 1898 (*Smrutichitre*, 844).

13. L. Tilak, *I Follow*, 177.

14. N. V. Tilak, *Bhakti*, 81; trans. Nicol Macnicol. These are the first three stanzas of the poem.

Chapter 6: Lakshmibai pp. 32–41

1. L. Tilak, *I Follow*, 153.

2. The thread ceremony is supposed to take place at different ages for boys of different castes, Brahmins receiving it at the earliest age. Traditionally it marked the initiation into instruction in the Vedas. Only the three higher castes have the ceremony, which is considered a rebirth. The three higher castes are thus the "twice-born" (*dvija*). Before receiving the thread the child is considered a Shudra, as technically all women always are (and thus the hearing of the Vedas is proscribed until after this ceremony takes place). There have always been many who did not wear the thread, Brahmins being the most diligent to do so. The thread is at least three strands, normally worn over the left shoulder and under the right arm, going diagonally across the chest to the right hip.

3. From Bruce, "Brahmin Woman," 836.

4. Ibid., 837.

5. Ashok Devdatt Tilak, *Agadi Step by Step* (Nasik, India: Mayawati A. Tilak, 1968), 26.

6. L. Tilak, *I Follow*, 191–92.

7. Ibid., 201.

8. "Mama is quite famous for her kirtans & for her lectures! She goes to Pandit Mrs. Hume! So practically she is gradually taking my place! In everything she undertakes to do she is very earnest, and puts all her heart and soul into it, that has made her as she is and that is going to help her further." (Letter to Dattu, 5 Sept. 1912; see below on *kirtans*; *pandit* was used as a verb as "to teach," generally meaning language instruction.)

9. Lakshmibai's birthdate is unknown, probably in 1868. She died on February 24, 1936.

10. Malcolm Nazareth analyzes and exposes the suggestion that Lakshmibai's conversion was merely a following of her husband in his review of the famous Marathi motion picture based on Lakshmibai's account of her life with Tilak. See "Mehta's Movie 'Smrutichitre': Postcolonial Feminist Construct? 'Hindutvavadi' Distortion?" *Religion and Society* 43, no. 3 (Sept. 1996): 70–113. A. D. Tilak also addresses these opinions in his introduction to *Sampurna Smrutichitre*, pointing out also that Lakshmibai gloried in being Tilak's student and wrote a poem about being the wife of a great poet (see pp. 13–15).

11. *Dnyanodaya* 64, 31 Aug. 1905, 35; translation added. This statement by Lakshmibai is difficult to reconcile with words spoken in 1933 in her president's address to the Marathi Christian Literary Conference. There Lakshmibai related how

> After becoming a Christian, for many years I would apply *kunku*. No missionary objected to this. Once, however, a learned Indian Christian lady connected *kunku* with the Shakta cult, misled me, and took a promise from me that I would never again apply *kunku*. Afterwards Tilak explained to me the meaning of *kunku*. But since I had given a promise I did not apply it again and Tilak never insisted that I do so. (*Smrutichitre*, 704)

Perhaps it was the very comments quoted above from *Dnyanodaya* that caused Tilak to point out to Lakshmibai that she had been misled; or perhaps Tilak at that time objected to *kunku* and only later changed his position, and Lakshmibai's memory failed in that detail.

12. A. D. Tilak, "Narayan," 20.

13. A. D. Tilak, *Agadi*, 46.

14. Winslow, *Tilak*, 26. In line with the realism of biblical biography it is surely not out of place to point out here that though Lakshmibai was truly freed from caste prejudice, she did not fully break

free of some fears related to aspects of Hindu belief. A. D. Tilak tells how his father's marriage in 1918 was arranged in the (for Hindus) forbidden second half of the month of Chaitra. For many months after the ceremony any news of a death was related by Lakshmibai to the fact that the marriage of her son had been performed in an inauspicious season. (See *Smrutichitre* page 12 for this and other examples.)

15. N. V. Tilak, *Bhakti*, 57; trans. JCW. Susila (or Sushila) is a girl's name.

Chapter 7: Christian Service pp. 42–55

1. L. Tilak, *I Follow*, 155.

2. Ibid., 133.

3. A. D. Tilak suggests there was a deeper reason in disagreements and quarrels within the mission (*Smrutichitre*, 322).

4. Tara was adopted in July 1900 but was treated as a true daughter to the point that her origin was never spoken of.

5. L. Tilak, *I Follow*, 213–14.

6. Ibid., 228.

7. Tilak acknowledged his over-generosity in a letter to a friend on 4 September 1903:

> You must have received my p[ost] c[ard]. It seems that you misunderstood me. I don't & never wished (*sic*) to ask you for any money. ...
>
> As to money, I shall be frank now. Today I have not a single pice in my home with a debt of about 150 rupees! How I reduced myself to this state! It is known to God, as a rule I don't care to give out what I did or do. I can only say that it was my foolishness in helping the needy during plague! Seven destitute patients were helped by me, each required on an average Rupees fifty! With no savings of my own, I simply got things on credit and gave them away to these. My wife, who did not approve of this, was much displeased, but oh! she is my wife a Mrs Tilak. God bless her, she knew the story of the "Vicar of Wakefield" and called me one, that is all. For my sake, keep this to yourself. I don't want to make myself known as a foolish giver & indeed I do not want to be one any more.
>
> Now I explain all this to you because, you may not say like men & women here that nowadays I am a slave of money. But of this debt, I believe I would revert to my natural attitude towards money & position.

8. *The Harvest Field*, 39, no. 6 (June 1919): 236–37.

9. A striking example of the power of Tilak's poetry is seen in an incident related by Rev. A. D. Ohal:

> Just recently I happened to sit in the railway carriage beside a Brahman priest of the highest order. When he new (*sic*) that I was a Christian, he moved a little so that his clothes did not touch mine. I was reading the Christian *bhajans* of Mr. Tilak, and said, "Here is a *bhajan* full of Sanskrit words some of which I do not understand; would you explain them to me?" He would not take the book in his hand, so I read it to him. I had not read two lines of the *bhajan* when he told me to stop, and half singing them after me he explained in his beautiful Marathi line after line till the last where the whole thought of the poem is summed up that without Christ we can never know God. He repeated it loud enough so that many people in that carriage could hear. I read five or six other *bhajans* to him, and he was so pleased with them that he wanted to know my address, and accepted my invitation to come and see me. ("Sholapur Station" in *Report of the American Marathi Mission, 1910*, ed. William Hazen [Ahmednagar], 55–64.)

10. Winslow, *Tilak*, 54.

11. *Dnyanodaya* 59, 16 Aug. 1900, 33. *Christi* did not run for more than a year and a half.

12. See *Dnyanodaya* 78, 22 May 1919, 21, and further discussion of this in chapter 10.

13. From a letter to Hattie Bruce written 28 April 1914.

14. L. Tilak, *I Follow*, 322.

15. Ibid., 349.

16. A. D. Tilak, "Narayan," 16.

17. Winslow, *Tilak*, 47. A letter of 19 February 1919 says "your preface to *Abhanganjali* [Tilak's collection of *abhangs* for publication] is fine, but the voice of the Lord comes to me, that you should make great sacrifice and omit from it everything that applauds or praises me." The title, meaning *A Handful of Abhangs*, suggests cupped hands offering the hymns in worship.

18. L. Tilak, *I Follow*, 342–43. Tilak saw the crippling nature of much missionary munificence, as seen in this story related by J. F. Edwards:

> When he [Tilak] was asked what part he would take in the dedication ceremony of the great church building at Ahmed-

nagar, he replied, "Let me weep in the pulpit, that the building is erected in such a way that the Indian church will not be able to maintain it. This is a gift, but one inconsistent with the strength and spirit of the Indian church" (*Dnyanodaya* 90, 7 May 1931, 19).

19. Winslow, *Tilak*, 60.

20. These pictures with these inscriptions are still displayed at the United Theological College in Pune.

21. L. Tilak, *I Follow*, 342. Personal communication to his son on 28 August 1916, includes these bitter but not inappropriate words written during plague days:

> Very sorry to tell you that most of our chicken-hearted Christians instead of showing Christ's benevolence and heroism in them have fled and hidden themselves in any available holes, though most of them are inoculated. And yet these men are talking of their great campaign, which aims at making all India Christ's! Shame!

A following letter of 2 September includes this insightful evaluation:

> Indian Christians are found everywhere very bad givers, and lacking in the spirit of self-sacrifice. The missionaries have failed owing to various reasons to give India real Indian Christians. They have killed all the Indian virtues in the Indian Christians, and have failed to supplant any pure Christian or Western virtue in their place. We need *Indian Christians*. I am praying for that, I live and die for that.

22. Winslow, *Tilak*, 107.

23. *Dnyanodaya* 58, 20 Apr. 1899, 16; translation added.

24. N. V. Tilak, *Bhakti*, 111; trans. JCW.

Chapter 8: Early Witness Among Hindus pp. 56–62

1. *Dnyanodaya* 54, 8 Aug. 1895, 32.

2. *Dnyanodaya* 55, 23 Jan. 1896, 4.

3. *Dnyanodaya* 53, 27 Dec. 1895, 52.

4. *Dnyanodaya* 59, 19 July 1900, 29.

5. *Dnyanodaya* 54, 10 Oct. 1895, 41, and 54, 12 Dec. 1895, 50.

6. *Dnyanodaya* 55, 13 Aug. 1896, 33.

7. *Dnyanodaya* 55, 30 July 1896, 31.

8. *Dnyanodaya* 63, 22 Sept. 1904, 48.

9. *Dnyanodaya* 54, 31 Oct. 1895, 44; translation added.

10. *Dnyanodaya* 71, 19 Dec. 1912, 51; translation added. See p. 74 here.

11. *Dnyanodaya* 54, 14 Mar. 1895, 11.

12. *Dnyanodaya* 72, 30 Jan. 1913, 5.

13. *Dnyanodaya* 71, 5 Dec. 1912, 49.

14. A. H. Clark, W. Hazen, and C. Bruce, eds., *Centennial Report of the American Marathi Mission* (Ahmednagar, 1913), 100–102.

15. Compare Vengal Chakkarai's prophetic critique of church union schemes in *Rethinking Christianity in India*, ed. D. M. Devasahayam and A. N. Sudarisanam (Madras: A. N. Sudarisanam, 1938), chap. V.

16. Winslow, *Tilak*, 59.

17. Note Tilak's comment that "I have always pointed out to all my Christian brothers and sisters how important *bhajan, kirtan, pravachan* [religious discourse] and *purana* have been in this country in religious practice and evangelism." (Translation added; from *Smrutichitre*, part 3, chap. 15.) Tilak considered the *Christayana* as a *purana*, to be recited with detailed exposition of every phrase.

18. Winslow, *Tilak*, 34.

19. *Dnyanodaya* 58, 19 Oct. 1899, 42.

20. *Dnyanodaya* 59, 9 Aug. 1900, 32.

21. *Dnyanodaya* 63, 28 Jan. 1904, 4.

22. N. V. Tilak, *Bhakti*, 113; trans. JCW. This is the refrain of a six stanza song, "Christ the Mother Guru."

Chapter 9: Finding Christ pp. 63–71

1. The deprived background of most Christians leads many Hindus to consider Christianity a religion only for the lower castes, while the low standard of spirituality in most churches adds a further stumbling block.

2. See Winslow, *Tilak*, 34, 35; L. Tilak, *I Follow*, 254.

3. L. Tilak, *I Follow*, 254–55.

4. *Dnyanodaya* 74, 2 Dec. 1915, 48.

5. See Pandita Ramabai, *A Testimony*, 9th ed. (Kedgaon: Ramabai Mukti Mission, 1968 [1907]); (cf. also S. M. Adhav, *Pandita Ramabai* [Madras: CISRS/CLS, 1979], 130ff). In May 1905 Tilak and Lakshmibai spent some weeks with Pandita Ramabai at Kedgaon. Ramabai published the first edition of *Bhajanasangraha*, Tilak's first hymn collection. Malcolm Nazareth has pointed out

that Lakshmibai's "cultural conversion" after which she refused to wear *kunku* (see page 40 and chapter 6 note 11) can be precisely dated to those days in Kedgaon. Is it possible that Ramabai's story influenced Tilak's interpretation of his own experience?

6. L. Tilak, *I Follow*, 123.

7. Winslow, *Tilak*, 22.

8. Interpreting the "second conversion" is complicated by ambiguous dating. The date of writing of the key piece of evidence, *Dnyanodaya* 74, 2 Dec. 1915, 48, is uncertain; the article may have been written even ten years before publication. Tilak there puts the experience "some seven or eight" years after his baptism, but Hattie Bruce whom he identifies left India in May of 1901, so that prayer experience happened six years at most after his baptism. Reports of Tilak's account of his spiritual pilgrimage at the time of his ordination (August 1904) make no mention of any "second conversion." Lakshmibai's account indicates a dating "some ten years" later, but this is a weak translation from the Marathi which actually says ten to twelve years later! Lakshmibai seems to be definitely referring to both the experience and the dating of it as something Tilak spoke of rather than her own interpretation, but she was writing her account some 30 years later (perhaps only some 20 years later than Tilak's references to the events). As indicated above, Lakshmibai clearly relates the second conversion to the change to Hindu forms in Tilak's expression of faith in Christ.

In a footnote in *Smrutichitre*, p. 374, A. D. Tilak quotes from a report on a Tilak message in south India in 1916 wherein the prayer with a missionary has the missionary referred to in masculine gender; but note that Tilak would have spoken in south India in genderless English, so the masculine was added in in translation and this should not be taken as a contradiction of Tilak's other account of the prayer encounter. Tilak here claims that it was particularly the fatherhood of God that he had never before understood, and this again militates against accepting his interpretation as quotes above indicate he had a clear grasp of this doctrine and its implications well before the prayer encounter with Hattie Bruce. But this at least shows that in 1916 Tilak still held to a belief that he was truly spiritually converted many years after his baptism.

9. Winslow, *Tilak*, 96.

10. Ibid., 101.

11. N. V. Tilak, *Bhakti*, 90; trans. Mrs. L. M. Edwards.

12. Nicol Macnicol highlighted this point:

He [N. V. Tilak], I believe, more than any other Indian Christian, has shown the Indian Church the way, and led her in the way, into one rich province of her own inheritance that she can possess in the name of Christ. What union with God means, and how it may be realized, this Church may well reveal with a new fullness to the world. If we compare the Marathi hymn-book with the hymn-books of the West we shall notice how many more hymns there are in the former on the subject of union and communion with God than in the latter. And for these the hymn-book is almost entirely indebted to N. V. Tilak. (Quoted from *The Making of Modern India* in J. F. Edwards, "How Far May Christianity Be Indianised? N. V. Tilak's Answer," *Dnyanodaya* 84, 21 May 1925, 21.)

13. N. V. Tilak, *Bhakti*, 4, 5, 6, 25, 32 (*Christayana* 1:7, 17, 26; 2:38, 88); trans. JCW.

14. N. V. Tilak, *Bhakti* 140; trans. Sister of the C.S.M.V. (Community of St. Mary the Virgin), an Anglican sisterhood.

Chapter 10: The Indian Heritage pp. 72–81

1. From Lakshmibai's story of her life with Tilak; *Smrutichitre*, part 3, chap. 15:456; translation added. *Pravachan* is religious discourse.

2. *Dnyanodaya* 76, 28 June 1917, 26. The entire Marathi service is printed in Appendix 6 of *Smrutichitre*, 753–64.

3. *Dnyanodaya* 57, 23 June 1898, 25. Notice also, however, Tilak's criticism of Sai Baba (Shirdi) *advaitins* in *Dnyanodaya* 73, 12 Nov. 1914, 46. He criticizes the inconsistency of worshipping Sai Baba when *advaita* leaves no place for a god to worship.

4. *Dnyanodaya* 72, 28 Aug. 1913, 35.

5. *Dnyanodaya* 69, 24 Nov. 1910, 47.

6. "The term 'Hindu' had originally a territorial and not a creedal significance. It implied residence in a well-defined geographical area. ... The differences among the sects of the Hindus are more or less on the surface, and the Hindus as such remain a distinct cultural unit, with a common history, a common literature and a common civilisation." S. Radhakrishnan, *The Hindu View of Life: Upton Lectures Delivered at Manchester College, Oxford, 1926* (London: George Allen & Unwin, 1939), 13–14. Tilak could even fit within the latter half of this definition of a Hindu.

7. *Dnyanodaya* 72, 31 July 1913, 31.

8. Tilak virtually arrived at this conclusion in the last stage of his life by welcoming unbaptized disciples of Christ into full "Christian" fellowship.

9. *Dnyanodaya* 72, 21 Aug. 1913, 34.

10. *Abhang* 160, quoted from Winslow, *Tilak*, 60.

11. See *Dnyanodaya* 76, 28 June 1917, 26. Note some adverse reaction to these views as a letter of 15 Sept. 1912, states that "My ... 'Study of Indian Myths' has exposed me to adverse criticism by some missionaries and Indian Christians whose religion is nothing but Churchianity and dogmas! Two great evils ever obstructing the way of the world to its Saviour Jesus Christ."

12. *Dnyanodaya* 71, 5 Sept. 1912, 37.

13. Winslow, *Tilak*, 56–57.

14. *Dnyanodaya* 59, 7 June 1900, 23.

15. *Dnyanodaya* 66, 17 Oct. 1907, 42.

16. *Dnyanodaya* 76, 24 May 1917, 21, *abhangs* 44 to 51.

17. Quoted from J. F. Edwards, in *Dnyanodaya* 84, 21 May 1925, 21.

18. This is especially striking in light of Jesus' clear words that it had been better for Judas had he never been born (Mt. 26:24).

19. If this is true of the Samaritan faith, which was so near the Jewish faith, it is inescapable that it applies equally to Hinduism.

20. Winslow, *Tilak*, 105.

21. Ibid., 61.

22. L. Tilak, *I Follow*, 316.

23. *Dnyanodaya* 78, 1 May 1919, 18.

24. *Dnyanodaya* 78, 1 May 1919, 18. See also 78:21 on *satyagraha* ("truth force"), and Jesus as the greatest *satyagrahi*.

25. *Dnyanodaya* 78, 22 May 1919, 21.

26. N. V. Tilak, *Bhakti*, 28–29 (*Christayana* 2:57–63); trans. JCW. "*Dharma* includes all the duties of religion; *artha* covers what we commonly call the material or secular sphere" (JCW's notes).

Chapter 11: Sannyasa pp. 82–98

1. L. Tilak, *I Follow*, 313, 334. The Tilak correspondence contains striking proof of Lakshmibai's statement that Tilak all through life sought growth and transformation. Note especially letters of 3 Dec. 1909 and 4 Nov. 1912, which show him praying for fresh power from the Holy Spirit.

2. It is tempting to think of Tilak (in line with western myths of the East) as the serene contemplative seer; but though he was a mystic

of a high order he was also a fiery prophet. Lakshmibai tells how "once when he was preaching ... his excitement rose to such heights that, as he spoke, he struck the table before him, and with that one blow the table was split" (L. Tilak, *I Follow*, 323).

3. N. V. Tilak, "The Educated Classes of India," in *Report of the American Marathi Mission 1908*, ed. R. A. Hume, H. G. Bissell, and A. H. Clark (Ahmednagar, 1909), 6–8.

4. From p. 12 in "Ahmednagar City," in *American Marathi Mission Report for 1914*, ed. L. S. Gates, R. S. Fose, and E. R. Bissell (Ahmednagar, 1915), 10–24.

5. Winslow, *Tilak*, 111–12. The Tilak correspondence does not presently contain this letter. A letter of 11 February refers to returning from Pune that day after a week away, so presumably 4 or 5 February 1916 must be the date of the event discussed. But this 11 February letter seems to assume that Dattu already knew about the new vision and path:

> I returned this afternoon from a week's trip to Bombay and Poona. I read your letter to Mama. I personally am going to stay in Fririkar's garden all by myself for at least a couple of months, partly that I might push on the *Christayana* with more zest and rapidity and partly that I might wait upon God and on Him alone for help [&] guidance in the new vision He has given me & the new path He has opened before me.

It seems the only way to fit these facts together is to suppose that Tilak wrote a letter between 4 and 11 February briefly telling of a life-changing encounter, which this 11 February letter refers to. Presumably Dattu asked for more details about the encounter and this elicited the March letter that Winslow quotes. However, the Winslow letter does not seem to presuppose such earlier communication so it must be considered possible that Winslow's date is wrong or that Tilak already was moving in a new direction when the train episode occurred.

6. Ibid., 112–13. The exact date is supplied from the correspondence as Winslow does not mention it. Much of the material from the 5 July letter can also be found in these pages in Winslow.

7. L. Tilak, *I Follow*, 343.

8. On the call to America see letters of 16 and 27 Dec. 1916, etc.

9. Some very brief extracts from letters must suffice to demonstrate this point.

To Dattu, June 30, 1911:

Have you yet written any letter to Ruth [Dattu's future wife]? Write at once, let it be simple, true and loving, and never *romantic*! Simple but earnest love wins a woman and teaches her to honour a man and confide in him. Don't wonder that I am telling you this. The father must help his child even in such matters. It is foolish and harmful not to do so. It is the father's duty. Write to Ruth regularly and write in such a way as you both become the best friends in the world, but write so as to increase your influence on her.

To Dattu, July 15, 1911:

It is good for you that you were not teased about studies in your childhood which was really longer in your case, that has given you very good physical and intellectual health. That is why you have in you to grasp art, science, and literature. You will be an all-round fellow one day, because you were so free to play and while away your time in your childhood.

To a counselor of Dattu, June 18, 1914:

In short I myself prefer that Dattu keeps on with his study of science, but I have never prevented him from following his own judgement by the mere use of parental authority, and in this case too I don't want to do so. My desire has been and will be to help him form a wise judgement.

To Dattu, Sept. 20, 1917:

I cannot help you worrying yourself in the way you have been doing. Please go on with your studies, have faith in God & have faith in me. I can say nothing more. Are you determined to do harm to yourself by uselessly imagining and magnifying difficulties? Nothing is impossible to God & through God to me. If you can't believe this, do please as you like. Don't listen to worldly minded ones who know me not, and who know not my Heavenly Father & His love and His Providence. You will be degenerated in spirit & faith if you are led by such. I don't want you to leave your course to go to Bombay, but to mind your studies. *I shall give you 100 rupees for your marriage* besides.

It must be noted here that Lakshmibai attributes Dattu's failure in his M.A. studies to the turmoil surrounding the birth of Tilak's new work (*I Follow*, 318).

10. Winslow, *Tilak*, 114. There is a definite pattern present in the visionary experiences of Tilak's life. Dreams helped motivate his baptism; a vision assisted his step to cease receiving mission funds

in 1904; this last vision was preceded by more than a year by another described in a letter of 2 June 1916 (this passage is highlighted as it is the only English section of an otherwise Marathi letter):

> Jesus actually came and locked me in an embrace last night. The touch of his holy bosom I could not bear. I shivered and trembled, but I felt myself to be in heaven. He spoke to me and separated me to go on a mission, which I am asked to keep to myself & let the world know from what he enabled me to do.

(Winslow clearly dates a vision in July or August of 1917, as in the text above, and it seems very unlikely that he could have been referring to this vision of June 1916, misdating it so badly; A. D. Tilak's research and the dates of *Dnyanodaya* poems about the 1917 vision confirm that Winslow is not mistaken and there were two different visions.) These last two visions related to the final step into a new ministry pattern. Tilak had some understanding of the costs involved in the steps he made following these experiences. Especially for the last step it seems possible that he sought out special motivations. In this light it is possible that the train encounter described above was not quite so crucial as Tilak himself tried to interpret it to be, and this might explain the chronology problem discussed in note 5 above. (That is, Tilak was already thinking of a new direction and took the train encounter as vindication and a point of description for others to grasp. A vision two months later still did not move him into action, but further study and reflection and another vision finally did result in action some 18 months after the train encounter.) This is not to suggest that a merely psychological interpretation suffices to explain away the visions. Tilak clearly had a dynamic personal relationship with the living Christ and these observations on his visionary experiences are not intended to cast any doubt on the reality of this relationship. The relationship between the psychological and the spiritual in visionary experience is a complex subject and these incidents from Tilak's life clearly provide important data for such considerations.

11. *Dnyanodaya* 76, 6 Sept. 1917, 36.

12. *Dnyanodaya* 76, 20 Sept. 1917, 38.

13. As the following paragraphs show, however, it was truly *sannyasa* that Tilak was entering. How he related this to his previous Hindu experience is clear from this undated letter (c. 1919):

> Now all *sansar* [worldly concern] is entirely made over to my son. ... It is not a new resolution in me. When a boy of 22 I ... renounced wife and father and all and went after the search of the truth. I was compelled to return home after 3 or 4 years by

the then my guru. I never enjoyed *sansar* [the world]. I always thought I was made to be far above it. Thus all my earnings practically belonged to the world and I don't remember to have ever accumulated any noticable (*sic*) treasure, though circumstances sometimes tempted me to try to do it.

Again after 11 years passed over my first attempt at renunciation, I heard the Voice asking me to follow Jesus. And this was my second renunciation.

Again in 1917 the same voice asked me to be free from human control and human aid and rely entirely on God; and that was my third renunciation.

It is not yet complete. I am dying to be able to say (with my Lord) to my wife "what have I to do with thee"; dying to say with him to say to myself and the world "whosoever shall do the will of my Father which is in heaven, the same is my mother, and sister and brother." I am dying to realize and experience with Paul "yet not I, but Christ liveth in me." I am not willing to be satisfied with whit less than what is promised by the Lord.

14. *Dnyanodaya* 76, 4 Oct. 1917, 40. (Translation added; also found in chap. 17 of part 3 of the full Marathi editions of *Smrutichitre*.)

15. Ibid.; translation added.

16. Ibid.; the passages were Col. 3:3, Acts 2:4, Rom. 8:35–39, Phil. 1:21, Mt. 5:11–12, Mt. 25:34–40, and 1 Cor. 13. If these things were worked out in a person's life he could be a Christian *sannyasi* with authority to speak like 1 Cor. 11:1. (This can also be found in chap. 17 of part 3 of the full Marathi editions of *Smrutichitre*.)

17. Winslow, *Tilak*, 119. (The translation of "God's *darbar*" is from H. Staffner, *The Significance of Jesus Christ in Asia* [Anand: Gujarat Sahitya Prakash, 1985], 150.)

18. Ibid., 118.

19. *Dnyanodaya* 77, 7 Mar. 1918, 10. (Translation added; also found in chap. 15 of part 3 of the full Marathi editions of *Smrutichitre*.)

20. Winslow, *Tilak*, 120. (This can also be found in chap. 15 of part 3 of the full Marathi editions of *Smrutichitre*.)

21. L. Tilak, *I Follow*, 326–27.

22. Mr. A. D. Tilak in conversation gave me the information that from his personal interviews with Christian members of the *darbar* there were also at least four or five Hindu members of the *darbar*, but he was never able to locate and interview any of them.

23. N. V. Tilak, *Bhakti*, 142; adaptation of the translation by C.S.M.V., in comparison with the Marathi original.

Chapter 12: Final Days pp. 99–103

1. L. Tilak, *I Follow*, 333.

2. Letter of 21 Feb. 1919.

3. See L. Tilak, *I Follow*, 335, 343 and letters of 21 Feb. and 7 Mar. 1919 from the Tilak correspondence.

4. L. Tilak, *I Follow*, 342.

5. Ibid., 345. The line from Tilak's song on his imperfection is as translated by J. C. Winslow, *Tilak*, 48. The phrase "No trouble ..." is as translated by J. C. Winslow, *Tilak*, 125. This passage from Lakshmibai's text seems to be a rearrangement of material from Tilak's 14 Aug. 1915 letter to R. A. Hume. A. D. Tilak suggests that Lakshmibai should not have referred to the quoted document as Tilak's will since it was not legally filed as such (*Smrutichitre*, 516).

6. Ibid., 346.

7. Ibid., 348.

8. Winslow, *Tilak*, 123.

9. Ibid., 124.

10. "We were surprised to see her courage," wrote Rev. John Malelu of Lakshmibai. Foundationless rumours were floated that Tilak at the end regretted having become a Christian, it seems due to his being cremated rather than buried (on this see *Smrutichitre*, 524).

11. L. Tilak, *I Follow*, 353.

12. N. V. Tilak, *Bhakti*, 140; trans. C.S.M.V.

Chapter 13: Epilogue pp. 104–107

1. Winslow, *Tilak*, 121.

2. The difficult issue of how the *darbar* related to the church is illustrated by the fact that "*darbar*" was not merely a name Tilak coined for his organization, but was in fact his chosen designation as an appropriate name for the church itself. In describing the meaning of a local *darbar* he suggests it is *swaaraajya*, which he calls the kingdom of God. (He coins a word, playing on Gandhi's familiar term for political freedom, *swaraajya*.) Misunderstanding and tensions between Tilak and the Christian community obviously resulted from such descriptions. (From untranslated material in *Smrutichitre*, part 3, chap. 15.)

3. That most Hindus are offended by baptism, which is understood as a sign of the abandonment of the Hindu community and rejection of Hindu culture, is understandable since most Christians understand and practice baptism in exactly this way.

4. N. V. Tilak, *Bhakti*, 114–15; 1st and 4th (last) stanzas; trans. JCW.

Glossary

abhang	See definition on page 49: a religious song or hymn written in the traditional meter used by Indian poet-saints to express their devotion to God.
advaita	Non-dualism or monism; the philosophical school that sees all reality as one, especially emphasizing the Upanishadic teaching that the human soul (*atman*) is not essentially different from the universal soul (*brahman*).
Alvars	South Indian (Tamil) poets who were devoted to the god Vishnu in his various manifestations.
anuraga	Attachment, love, loyalty.
ashram	1. A retreat center; traditionally a hermitage for ascetics. 2. A stage in the life of a high caste Hindu (see *sannyasa*).
Ati-shudras	A reference to outcastes or untouchables; those "beyond the Shudras."
Bengal	Eastern India, now divided into Bangladesh and West Bengal state of India.
Bhagavad Gita	A section of the Mahabharata epic, often printed separately and esteemed as the greatest Hindu scripture. Dated between 200 B.C. and A.D. 200
bhajan	A spiritual song sung repetitiously.
bhakta	A devotee.
bhakti	Devotion, worship. (The most popular of the traditional three ways to attain salvation.)
Brahman	1. The universal soul (also spelled *Brahma*). 2. A personal manifestation of the universal soul, especially known as Brahma the Creator.

Brahmin	The highest of the castes of Hinduism, traditionally priests (sometimes spelled *Brahman*).
caste	A social division mentioned in the Vedas that at later stages developed into a rigid hierarchy based on birth. Two Sanskrit terms are translated as caste though their meanings are quite different. There are four castes (Sanskrit *varna*): Brahmin (priestly castes), Kshatriya (soldier castes), Vaisya (merchant castes), and Shudra (menial working castes). Many not even ranking as Shudras were considered outcastes. In practical out-working castes (Sanskrit *jati*) are innumerable, as subdivisions are at least as important as the broad and largely theoretical delineation of the four *varnas*.
Chaitanya	A devotee of Krishna who spearheaded a *bhakti* revival in Bengal in the early 16th century.
Christayana	Tilak's epic poem on the life of Christ; the "goings" (*ayana*) of Christ.
darbar	Royal court. Used by Tilak for his brotherhood and for the church.
darbari	Member of a *darbar*; here a member of Tilak's new brotherhood.
dasa	Servant or slave; Tilak's self-designation in his *abhangs* (songs, hymns).
Deccan	The plateau region of southern India.
diksha	An initiatory rite; consecration for religious ends.
Dnyaneswara	The first of the great Marathi poet-saints, born around A.D. 1275.
Dnyanodaya	"Rise of Knowledge," weekly magazine of the American Marathi Mission. See *jñana* (modern spelling).
Gujerat	The area of western India north of Maharashtra, presently an Indian state (now Gujarat).
guru	A teacher, in the highest spiritual sense often considered and treated as a god.
jñana	Knowledge; spiritual insight, especially as procured by meditation. (One of the three traditional ways to attain salvation.)
jñani	One who practices and achieves *jñana*.
karma	1. In the general sense, good works; religious, moral and caste duties. (One of the three traditional ways to attain salvation.)

2. The principle that reward or punishment infallibly follows every deed. At times the recompense comes in the present life; always the situation and fate of the coming life are determined by one's karma.

kirtan   A religious service. See the definition on page 61.

kunku   Red powder applied to the forehead especially by married women.

Mahabharata   The great epic poem of India, consisting of 110,000 couplets. Broadly a story of a civil war in north India, but touching every aspect of life. Traditionally authorship is ascribed to Vyasa, but clearly the epic developed and grew under many hands; generally dated between 400 B.C. to A.D. 400.

Maharashtra   State in western India whose greatest city is Mumbai (the legal name now for Bombay).

mahatma   Literally, great (*maha*) soul (*atma*).

mantra   A verse of Vedic scripture, often of mystic meaning and considered to have great power.

Marathi   The language of Maharashtra, derived from Sanskrit in the Indo-European family of languages.

Maruti   Another name for Hanuman, the monkey god who loyally serves Ram in the Ramayana.

Mussulman   Older terms for a Muslim, a follower of the Islamic
Mahomadan   faith.

Nanak   Early 16th century founder of the Sikh religion, which is part of the *bhakti* movements across north India.

Narayan   One of many names of the god Vishnu, who incarnated himself primarily as Ram (Rama) and Krishna.

Nayanars   South Indian (Tamil) poets devoted to the god Shiva.

outcastes   People and groups never brought officially into relationship with Vedic culture or who for various reasons were considered unclean. Also called untouchables or *panchamas*; more recently called *harijans* (children of God) or scheduled castes and now most frequently *dalits* (the oppressed).

Pandharpur   The west Indian (Maharashtrian) city which is the center for the popular Hinduism espoused by the Marathi poet-saints.

pandit(a)   A scholar or learned man or woman.

Parsi (Parsee)	A follower of the Zoroastrian faith.
Punjab	A fertile area in northwestern India, now divided between India and Pakistan.
Puranas	Late (A.D. 600 to 1600) Sanskrit scriptures containing innumerable myths and legends, some of which are ancient; 18 major and 18 minor Puranas are traditionally referred to, but there is no agreed classification of these works.
Ram, Rama	The hero of the Ramayana, apparently an historical figure who grew into popular recognition as an incarnation of the god Vishnu.
Ramayana	The epic poem telling of Rama and his wife Sita. Valmiki was the original author around 300 B.C. The myth developed over later centuries and the retelling by Tulsidas (the 16th century A.D. *Ramcharitmanas*) is more widely known and esteemed in north India than Valmiki's original. Reinterpretations, especially orally, continue to the present time.
rishi	A sage; a patriarch possessed of great power and/or wisdom.
rupee	Indian currency, presently about 42 rupees to U.S. $1.
sadhu	A broad term for an ascetic or holy man.
sahib	"Master"; a term that came to be almost universally applied to westerners.
Samajists	A generic term referring to members of a society or assembly (*samaj*). The late 19th century Arya Samaj sought a return to the Vedas, while the Prarthana and Brahmo Samajes propagated a reformed theistic Hindu faith.
sampradaya	"Tradition." Also the community that upholds a traditional teaching and way of life; thus often translated as "sect" (religious order or denomination).
Sampurna Smrutichitre	"complete" *Smrutichitre* ("Memory-pictures"), Lakshmibai's title for her story of life with Tilak.
sannyasa	Traditionally the fourth and last stage of life for a high caste Hindu, the others being *brahmacharya* (student), *grihasthya* (householder or family man), and *vanaprasthya* (recluse for meditation). In *sannyasa* everything is renounced, including family, caste status and worship of idols. This is final preparation for death, breaking all earthly bonds in advance. Rarely was this ideal of a four-stage life practiced.

sannyasi(n)	Technically, one in *sannyasa*, but often the term is used more loosely like *sadhu*.
sanskara	Religious purificatory rite; 16 Hindu *sanskaras* are generally listed but few Hindus practice more than half of these.
Sanskrit	The Indo-European language of the Hindu scriptures, still spoken by some *pandits*.
satyagraha	"Truth force." Gandhi's name for the nonviolent resistance movement aimed at winning over a foe by enduring undeserved suffering, which he applied against the British Raj.
shakti/shakta	*Shakti* is literally "power," but is also a generic term for the many manifestations of the Goddess (Kali, Durga, Parvati, etc.). A *shakta* is a devotee of the Goddess, in whatever form. Shaktism (or Tantrism) has two broad divisions, one of which involves normally forbidden or even revolting practices intentionally undergone in an effort to transcend (apparent) practical reality.
Shankaracharya	Shankara (c. 9th century A.D.) is the best known proponent of *advaita* vedanta philosophy; *acharya* means spiritual guide or teacher and is a not uncommon honorific title. A succession of Shankaracharyas continues to the present time at centers (traditionally four, but five claim the heritage) established by Adi (first) Shankaracharya.
Shastras	A general word for various Hindu religious books.
Shiva	God the Destroyer in the commonly quoted triadic scheme of Brahma (Creator), Vishnu (Preserver) and Shiva (Destroyer). To the devotee of Shiva, however, he is creator, preserver and destroyer and an ocean of grace and mercy.
Shudra	The fourth caste; traditionally not permitted to know the higher teachings of Hinduism nor even to enter the temples of the higher castes. Often difficult to distinguish from outcastes.
swaraajya *swaaraajya*	Sovereignty, independent dominion, self-rule; the first spelling is the Gandhian term used for self-rule or independence for India from Britain; the latter spelling (differently pronounced, from rather obscure Sanskrit roots) was used by Tilak for God's sovereign rule or kingdom.

Tamil	The Dravidian language of the present southeastern Indian state of Tamil Nadu, an ancient and important language and culture.
Tukaram	Generally acknowledged as the greatest of the Marathi Hindu poet-saints, born around 1608 and died (by tradition was taken bodily up to heaven) in 1649.
Upanishads	A collection of mystical and philosophical writings; 108 are traditionally recognized, but 13 are generally held to be the oldest and most authoritative. These are the end of the Vedic canon.
Vaisya	The third caste, traditionally businessmen of various types.
Vedas	The most ancient of Hindu scriptures. In the broader meaning the Vedas are: Hymns (often referred to as Vedas in the more narrow meaning), the Brahmanas (mainly rituals and *mantras* for the priests [Brahmins]), and the Upanishads.
Vedanta	The dominant school of Indian philosophy, of which *advaita* is one sub-school. Literally means "end of the Vedas," taken to mean the culmination of the Vedas or as a reference to the Upanishads as the last section of the Vedas, from which the Vedanta philosophies are primarily developed.
vedantin	A follower of Vedanta philosophy.
viraga	Indifference to (detachment from) the things of this world; passionlessness.
Vishnu	God the Preserver in the commonly quoted triadic scheme of Brahma (Creator), Vishnu (Preserver) and Shiva (Destroyer). Much more significantly, Vishnu is supreme God (creator, preserver and destroyer) for the majority of Hindus. He in mercy "incarnates" repeatedly, most importantly as Rama and Krishna.
yoga	In general usage, deep contemplation or meditation. In more technical usage, one of various methods of physical discipline and meditation through which total self-control or God-realization is acquired. Etymologically, the act of yoking or joining. Also one of the six orthodox schools of Hindu philosophy.

References Cited

Abbott, Justin E., trans.
  1929 *Stotramala: A Garland of Hindu Prayers*. The Poet-Saints of
        Maharashtra, No. 6. Pune, India: Scottish Mission Industries.

Adhav, S. M.
  1979 *Pandita Ramabai*. Confessing the Faith in India Series, No.
        13. Madras: CISRS/CLS.

Bruce, Hattie L.
  n.d.   "Sketch of a Brahmin Woman," in *Sampurna Smrutichitre*,
        by Lakshmi Tilak, ed. A. D. Tilak, 831–39. Mumbai: Popular
        Prakashan.

Clark, A. H., W. Hazen, and C. Bruce, eds.
  1913 *Centennial Report of the American Marathi Mission*. Ahmed-
        nagar.

Devadoss, D.
  1946 *Life of Poet H. A. Krishna Pillai*. Madras, India: The Madras
        Law Journal Press.

Devasahayam, D. M., and A. N. Sudarisanam, eds.
  1938 *Rethinking Christianity in India*. Madras: A. N. Sudarisanam.

Farquhar, J. N.
  1915 *The Crown of Hinduism*. Oxford: Oxford University Press.

Gates, L. S., R. S. Fose, and E. R. Bissell, eds.
  1915 *American Marathi Mission Report for 1914*. Ahmednagar.

Hazen, William, ed.
  1911 *Report of the American Marathi Mission, 1910*. Ahmednagar.

Hewat, E. G. K.
  1953 *Christ and Western India*. Bombay: Wilson College.

Hodge, J. Z.
  1939 "The Forward Movement in Evangelism under the N.C.C.,"
        in *Evangelism*, The Madras Series, vol. 3, Records of the
        International Missionary Council, Dec. 12–29, 1938, 80–122.
        New York: International Missionary Council.

Hume, R. A., H. G. Bissell, and A. H. Clark, eds.
  1909 *Report of the American Marathi Mission, 1908*. Ahmednagar.

Jacob, P. S.
  1979 *The Experiential Response of N. V. Tilak*. Confessing the
        Faith in India Series, No.14. Madras: CISRS/CLS.

Macnicol, Nicol
  1924 *The Making of Modern India*. Oxford: Oxford University Press.

Mueller, F. Max, ed.
  1878–1910 *Sacred Books of the East*. Oxford: Oxford University
        Press.

Nazareth, Malcolm
  1996 "A Tribute to Rev. N. V. Tilak after His Baptismal Centenary,"
        Vidyajyoti Journal of Theological Reflection 60, no. 6,7
        (June, July): 399–417, 443–54.

  1996 "Mehta's Movie 'Smrutichitre': Postcolonial Feminist
        Construct? 'Hindutvavadi' Distortion?" *Religion and Society*
        43, no. 3 (Sept. 1996): 70–113.

Radhakrishnan, S.
  1939 *The Hindu View of Life: Upton Lectures Delivered at
        Manchester College, Oxford, 1926*. London: George Allen
        & Unwin.

Ramabai, Pandita
  1968 [1907] *A Testimony*, 9th ed. Kedgaon, India: Ramabai Mukti
        Mission.

Sharpe, E. J.
  1965 *Not to Destroy But to Fulfil: The Contribution of J. N. Far-
        quhar to Protestant Missionary Thought in India before 1914*.
        Lund, Sweden: CWK Gleerup.

  1977 *Faith Meets Faith: Some Christian Attitudes to Hinduism in
        the Nineteenth and Twentieth Centuries*. London: SCM Press.

Staffner, H.
  1985 *The Significance of Jesus Christ in Asia*. Anand, India: Gujarat
        Sahitya Prakash.

Stietencron, Heinrich von
  1991 "Hinduism: On the Proper Use of a Deceptive Term," in
        Hinduism Reconsidered, ed. Gunther D. Sontheimer and

Hermann Kulke, Heidelberg University South Asian Studies, 24. New Delhi: Manohar Publications.

Tilak, Ashok Devdatt
1968 *Agadi Step by Step*. Nasik, India: Mayawati A. Tilak.

1978 "Narayan Waman Tilak," unpublished paper.

Tilak, Lakshmibai
1950 *I Follow After*, tr. E. Josephine Inkster. Madras: Oxford University Press.

1956 *From Brahma to Christ*. London: Lutterworth Press.

1989 *Sampurna Smrutichitre*, edited with introductions, footnotes and appendices by A. D. Tilak. Mumbai: Popular Prakashan.

Tilak, Narayan Vaman
n.d. *Bhakti Niranjana*. Nasik, India: Nagarik Press.

Winslow, Jack C.
1930 [1923] *Narayan Vaman Tilak: The Christian Poet of Maharashtra*, Builders of Modern India. Calcutta: Association Press.

World Missionary Conference
1910 *The Missionary Message in Relation to Non-Christian Religions*, Report of Commission IV, Edinburgh 1910. London: Oliphant, Anderson & Ferrier.

Recommended Reading

Klostermaier, Klaus K.
1994 *A Survey of Hinduism*. Albany: State University of New York Press.

Richard, H. L.
1997 "A Survey of Protestant Evangelistic Efforts among High Caste Hindus in the Twentieth Century," *Missiology* 25, no. 4 (Oct.): 419–45. *See bibliography for further reading*.

Staffner, Hans
1988 *Jesus Christ and the Hindu Community: Is a Synthesis of Hinduism and Christianity Possible?* Anand, India: Gujarat Sahitya Prakash.

Subbamma, B. V.
1970 *New Patterns in Discipling Hindus*. Pasadena, Calif.: William Carey Library.

Index